THE
WOMAN'S CLUB
OF
NASHVILLE
COOKBOOK

THE
WOMAN'S CLUB
OF
NASHVILLE
COOKBOOK

FAVORITE RECIPES
FROM THE
KITCHEN

compiled by the members of
The Woman's Club of Nashville

COOL
SPRINGS
PRESS

Library of Congress Cataloging-in-Publication Data

Woman's Club of Nashville.
    The Woman's Club of Nashville cookbook: favorite recipes from the kitchen/compiled by the members of the Woman's Club of Nashville.
  — [2nd ed.]
      p.   cm.
    First ed. published 1922.
    Includes index.
    ISBN 1-888608-87-0
    1. *Cookery, American.* I. Title.
TX715.W87257 1998
641.5973—dc21   98-43869
                                     CIP

First printing 1998
Printed in the United States of America
10 9 8 7 6 5 4 3 2 1

Cool Springs Press, Inc.
2020 Fieldstone Parkway
Suite 900210
Franklin, TN 37069

Dedicated to all the ladies before us who
have helped make our city a better place
in which to live

∽ CONTENTS ∽

Introduction
9

Appetizers and Beverages
13

Soups and Salads
31

Entrées
55

Vegetables and Side Dishes
95

Breads
121

Desserts
143

Extras
221

Index
234

The Woman's Club of Nashville

In 1908 a small group of young women met to talk about how they might make Nashville a better place to live. They were interested in educational and civic programs, and they decided to form a club that would allow them to pursue these interests.

The organizational meeting was held on May 20, 1909, on Forrest Avenue in "Edgefield Historic East Nashville." The East Nashville Civic Club was one of the first woman's civic clubs in Tennessee. Its first president was Mrs. Y.W. Haley (Leah), who served four years as president and continued her interest in the Club throughout her lifetime.

The members of the club adopted a creed:

> **"I believe in pure water, pure milk, pure food. I believe in the highest ideals for my community, specifically that health, music, art, love and work are ours to enjoy."**

They chose the red rose as their emblem and "Service" as their motto.

The women believed in the importance of intellectual development and enrichment. One of the club's first accomplishments was the securing of three branch libraries from the Carnegie Foundation.

The women were also concerned about the physical health of their families and others. It was through their efforts that the following were accomplished:

- The Smoke Abatement Law was enacted; it is still on the books.

- Regulations to help eliminate flies were adopted, such as wrapping bread, keeping meat under glass, and screening houses.

- Food and care were furnished for children who would not have had it otherwise. To accomplish this, members of the Civic Club worked through the East Nashville Milk and Ice Association. From these beginnings came "The McNeilly Day Home."

During World War I, members gave generously of their time, talent, and energy to the war effort. When peace arrived, the "East Nashville Civic Club" changed its name to "East Nashville Woman's Club" and branched into twenty-one departments.

A membership drive all over the city brought the membership to 1,000, and the club's name was changed to "The Nashville Woman's Club." Members wanted their young daughters to become interested in the club and its work, so they organized a Junior Department.

There were now members living in all parts of the city, and they dreamed of owning their own clubhouse. They purchased the former home of the Ridley Wills family at 217 Louise Avenue and made it the home of their club— now called "The Woman's Club of Nashville."

The Club was chartered on July 16, 1931, with this mission:

> **"The purpose of the corporation is to bring into helpful communication women interested in educational and civic progress, protection of youth, literary studies and homemaking."**

Pearl Harbor Day turned the members to war and Red Cross work, and they sold $200,000 worth of war bonds and stamps.

Together with the Nashville Fire Department, the Club's Welfare Department sponsored a clean-up, paint-up, fix-up campaign. Afterwards the City Beautiful Commission was enacted into law.

Club members began to dream of a larger home. They learned that a Colonial house at 3206 Hillsboro Road, the former home of Judge and Mrs. John Beauregard Daniel, had become available. They purchased this house and moved into it on November 14, 1957.

As large as this lovely house was, club members soon realized they needed more space for their many activities, and the Building Committee set to work. The membership voted that monies from Life Memberships would be credited to the Building Fund from 1969 to 1971, and many members purchased these memberships; the fund grew as a result of other activities as well.

On December 5, 1977, club leaders signed a contract to begin work on an auditorium. The membership chose to name this addition the Leah Herbert Haley Hall, in honor of their beloved first president, and the hall was dedicated on September 24, 1978.

"Keep On Keeping On" was another motto adopted by the club. The Woman's Club of Nashville continues to look to the future and will continue to "Keep On Keeping On."

The first *Woman's Club Cook Book* was published in Nashville in 1922. A page in the front matter of the book reads: *"This cook book contains a goodly number of tested and successful recipes contributed by members of the Woman's Club."*

Club members dreamed of creating another cookbook for many years. On pages 232–233 are the names of the members who contributed their own tested and successful recipes to today's cookbook. A "goodly number" of wonderful recipes that came out of the kitchen of the Woman's Club are also included, and they are marked with this icon:

WCN

Appetizers
and
Beverages

Oysters

Bury small oysters in ice until needed. Have the tall slender glasses in which they are to be served laid in the ice also, that they may be thoroughly chilled. Make a sauce of 2 tablespoons tomato catsup, 12 drops tabasco sauce, the juice of 1 lemon, a saltspoon of grated horse radish and a dash each of salt and paprika. Add 2 tablespoons of oyster liquor, mix thoroughly, and set on the ice until very cold. Put 5 oysters in the bottom of each chilled glass, pour the sauce upon them and serve.

Mrs. R. H. Tudor

Recipe from WCN Cookbook of 1922

☙ Crescent Roll Appetizers ❧

1 package refrigerated crescent roll dough
1 (8-ounce) package cream cheese
½ cup mayonnaise or ⅓ cup salad dressing (Miracle Whip)
3 rounded teaspoons (½ package) Hidden Valley dressing mix
1 quart diced fresh vegetables (broccoli, cauliflower, celery, carrots, etc.)

Preheat oven to 350 degrees. Divide crescent roll dough into 4 rectangles and place on a cookie sheet. Flatten slightly. Bake for 15 minutes. Be careful not to overbake. While the rectangles are cooling, mix cream cheese, mayonnaise, and dressing mix until smooth. Spread mixture on cooled rectangles and sprinkle with vegetables. Cut into 2-by-4-inch pieces (a pizza cutter works well for this).

☙ Olive Balls ❧

1 (5-ounce) jar bacon cheese spread
4 tablespoons margarine
Dash hot pepper sauce
Dash Worcestershire sauce
¾ cup flour
Small jar stuffed olives

Preheat oven to 400 degrees. Combine the bacon cheese spread, margarine, hot pepper sauce, Worcestershire sauce, and flour. Mix well. Mold 1 teaspoon of mixture around each olive. Place on an ungreased baking sheet. Bake for 12 to 15 minutes.

❧ Cheese Bites ❧

1 cup grated sharp Cheddar
cheese, softened to room
temperature
1 stick margarine, softened to
room temperature

½ cup flour
1 cup crispy rice cereal
½ teaspoon salt
½ teaspoon Worcestershire sauce

Preheat oven to 325 degrees. Combine all ingredients and mix thoroughly. Roll into ¾-inch balls and bake for 10 to 15 minutes.

❧ Cheese and Onion Canapés ❧

Desired number of small bread or
toast rounds
Onion, sliced thin

Mayonnaise
Parmesan or sharp Cheddar
cheese

Preheat oven to broil. Cover the bread rounds with thin slices of onion. Spread onion with mayonnaise and sprinkle with cheese. Broil rounds on a baking sheet until brown.

☜ Brie Appetizer ☞

1/4 cup finely chopped pecans
1/4 cup Kahlua or other coffee-
    flavored liqueur

3 tablespoons brown sugar
1 (14-ounce) package mini Brie
    Melba toast or crackers

Spread pecans in a 9-inch pie plate; microwave at high for
4 to 6 minutes, stirring every 2 minutes, until toasted. Add
Kahlua and brown sugar; stir well. Remove rind from top of
Brie; discard rind. Place Brie on a microwave-safe serving
plate. Spoon pecan mixture over top of Brie. Microwave
uncovered at high for $1^1/2$ to 2 minutes or until Brie softens
to desired consistency, giving dish a half turn after 1 minute.
Serve with Melba toast or crackers. Makes 12 servings.

☜ Deviled Ham and Cheese Snacks ☞

7 slices Pepperidge Farms
    sandwich bread, crust removed
2 (4½-ounce) cans deviled ham
1 (8-ounce) package cream
    cheese, at room temperature
1 egg yolk, beaten
1/2 teaspoon baking powder

2 teaspoons fresh grated onion
1 (8-ounce) can chopped water
    chestnuts
Dash salt
Dash hot pepper sauce
Paprika to taste

Cut each slice of bread into 4 squares. Spread thinly with
deviled ham. Mix together well the cream cheese, egg yolk,
baking powder, onion, water chestnuts, salt, and hot pepper
sauce. Drop a rounded teaspoon of the cheese mixture on top
of each bread square. Freeze. Remove from freezer about
30 minutes before baking. Preheat oven to 375 degrees. Sprinkle
squares with paprika. Bake on cookie sheet for about 20
minutes. Makes 28 squares.

∞ Greek Cheese Triangles ∞

½ pound Feta cheese, crumbled
½ pound Ricotta cheese
1 tablespoon minced parsley, dill,
    or chives

9 slices thin sandwich bread, crust
    removed

Preheat oven to 450 degrees. Blend together the Feta cheese, Ricotta cheese, and parsley, dill, or chives. Spread the mixture on bread slices. Bake for 10 to 15 minutes or until cheese melts. Cut each slice diagonally into 4 triangles. Serve warm. Makes 36 pieces.

∞ Cocktail Oyster Crackers ∞

1 package buttermilk dressing mix
2 tablespoons dill weed
¼ teaspoon garlic powder

1 cup vegetable oil
1 large box oyster crackers

Mix together the dressing mix, dill weed, garlic powder, and oil. In a large bowl, pour the mixture over oyster crackers. Let set for 3 hours, stirring occasionally.

☙ Oyster Cracker Munchies ❧

1 package ranch dressing mix
1 teaspoon dill weed
Pinch garlic powder
2 teaspoons lemon pepper

1 cup vegetable oil
1 (12-ounce) package oyster
   crackers

Preheat oven to 200 degrees. Combine the dressing mix, dill weed, garlic powder, lemon pepper, and oil; mix well. Pour mixture over the oyster crackers. Place in broiler pan. Bake for 1 hour, stirring every 20 minutes.

☙ Ranch Pinwheels ❧

1 package ranch dressing mix
2 (8-ounce) packages cream
   cheese
2 green onions, minced
4 (12-inch) flour tortillas

1 (3.8-ounce) can sliced black
   olives
1 (4-ounce) can diced green chiles
1 (4-ounce) jar pimentos

Mix together the dressing mix, cream cheese, and green onions. Spread mixture on the tortillas. Drain and blot dry the olives, chiles, and pimentos. Sprinkle the vegetables on top of the cream cheese mixture. Roll up tortillas tightly. Refrigerate for at least two hours. Cut tortillas into 1/2-inch spirals.
Makes 2 to 3 dozen pinwheels.

⏇ Open-Faced Ham Biscuits ⏇

1 pound cooked smoked ham
1 cup mayonnaise
¼ cup minced scallions
¼ cup minced fresh parsley
  leaves

1½ tablespoons Dijon-style
  mustard
1 tablespoon tomato paste
Pepper to taste
Approximately 10 biscuits, halved

Preheat oven to 400 degrees. In a food processor, grind the ham till fine. Transfer to a bowl. Add the mayonnaise, scallions, parsley, mustard, tomato paste, and pepper. Stir until well blended. Put in a pastry bag fitted with a large fluted tip. Pipe ham mixture onto biscuit halves. Heat in the middle of oven for 4 to 5 minutes. Makes approximately 20 open-faced ham biscuits.

⏇ Ham and Cheese Rolls ⏇

1 cup butter, softened
3 tablespoons poppy seeds
1 tablespoon Worcestershire sauce
3 tablespoons Grey Poupon
  mustard

1 small onion, grated
2 packages Pepperidge Farm Party
  Rolls
½ pound Swiss cheese, grated
½ pound thinly sliced lunch ham

Preheat oven to 400 degrees. Combine the butter, poppy seeds, Worcestershire sauce, mustard, and onion. Split each roll lengthwise. Spread butter mixture on cut sides of roll. Layer ham and cheese on one half of roll. Place other half of roll on top. Bake for 10 to 15 minutes. Makes 40 rolls.

☙ Congealed Corned Beef Spread ❧

2 cups boiling water
1 package lemon-flavored gelatin
1 beef bouillon cube
½ teaspoon Worcestershire sauce
1 (12-ounce) can corned beef
1 medium onion, finely chopped

3 boiled eggs, chopped (optional)
1½ cups diced celery
1 cup salad dressing
Assorted crackers
Lettuce leaf
Dollop of mayonnaise

Dissolve the gelatin in the boiling water. Add the beef bouillon cube and Worcestershire sauce. Stir until the cube dissolves. Let cool. Sliver the corned beef thin; run between fingers until every lump disappears. Blend the corned beef, onion, eggs, celery, and salad dressing. Gradually add the gelatin mixture. Pour into a greased 8-by-8-inch casserole dish. Chill. Serve with assorted crackers on a lettuce leaf with a dollop of mayonnaise on top. *This spread is better if made a day ahead. For best results, use the very best canned corned beef.*

☙ Spinach-Crab Dip ❧

1 (10-ounce) package frozen
  chopped spinach
1 tablespoon butter
1 small onion, chopped
1 pound crab meat
2 (8-ounce) packages cream
  cheese

1 (3-ounce) package cream cheese
1 tablespoon lemon juice
1 tablespoon hot pepper sauce
Sprinkle of garlic powder
Chips

Cook spinach in a small amount of water; let water cook out. Sauté the onion in the butter; do not brown. Mix remaining ingredients until well blended. Add the spinach and onion; mix well. Serve from a chafing dish with chips. *This is a delicious dip—and so easy to make!*

21

∽ Dawn's Apricot Cream Cheese Log ∽

1 (8-ounce) package cream
cheese, softened
2 tablespoons apricot jam
1 teaspoon vanilla

1 tablespoon sugar
15 apricots, cut fine
Finely chopped nuts
Wheat Thins or butterfly crackers

Blend together the cream cheese, jam, vanilla, and sugar until creamy. Mix in the apricots. Form a log; roll in the chopped nuts. Chill thoroughly. Serve with Wheat Thins or butterfly crackers. *This also makes a good filler for party sandwiches.*

∽ Shrimp Dip ∽

1 (3-ounce) package cream
cheese, softened
½ cup mayonnaise
½ cup chopped green pepper
½ cup chopped celery

½ cup chopped onion
1 small can tiny shrimp, drained
Cocktail sauce
Crackers

Mix together the cream cheese, mayonnaise, green pepper, celery, and onion until well blended. Add the shrimp; form into a log or ball. Chill well. When ready to serve, pour cocktail sauce over top of log or ball. Serve with crackers. *Do not use a blender to mix the ingredients.*

◌ Artichoke Dip ◌

1 (14-ounce) can artichokes, chopped
1 cup fresh shredded Parmesan cheese
½ cup mayonnaise
½ cup sour cream
Dash garlic powder
Green onions (optional)

Preheat oven to 350 degrees. Combine all ingredients. Pour into a casserole dish; bake for 30 minutes.

◌ Hot Chipped Beef Dip ◌

2 tablespoons butter
½ cup chopped pecans
Salt to taste
1 (8-ounce) package cream cheese, softened
2 tablespoons milk
1 (2½-ounce) jar dried beef, minced
1 cup sour cream
2 tablespoons minced onion
2 tablespoons minced green pepper
½ teaspoon garlic salt
½ teaspoon pepper
Crackers, corn chips, or toast strips

Preheat oven to 350 degrees. Melt the butter in a small skillet. Sauté the pecans in the butter. Add salt to taste and set aside. Blend together the cream cheese and milk; add the dried beef, sour cream, onion, green pepper, garlic salt, and pepper. Mix well. Turn into a lightly buttered small casserole. Top with the pecans. Bake for 20 minutes. Serve hot with crackers, corn chips, or toast strips.

✂ Spinach Dip ✂

1 package chopped spinach, thawed
¾ cup mayonnaise
¼ teaspoon beau monde
¾ cup sour cream

Dash hot pepper sauce
Garlic salt to taste
Lemon juice to taste
Corn chips or melba toast

Press thawed uncooked spinach between paper towels to remove all moisture. Mix spinach with remaining ingredients. Serve with corn chips or melba toast. Makes 2½ cups. *This dip can be prepared a day ahead.*

✂ Summer Salsa ✂

2 cans whole tomatoes
1 bunch green onions
½ yellow onion
Juice of 1 lemon
Juice of 1 lime
Jalapeño pepper and juice to taste

¼ to ½ cucumber
1 green tomato
1 teaspoon sugar
Salt and pepper to taste
Tortilla chips

Chop all ingredients; combine and mix well. Chill for at least 2 hours. Serve with tortilla chips. *If desired, you may substitute green chiles for the jalapeños.*

↷ Black-Eyed Pea Salsa ↶

1 can black-eyed peas, drained
2 tomatoes, chopped
1 small bunch green onions
3 tablespoons lime juice
1 tablespoon fresh cilantro,
   chopped

1 clove garlic, chopped
1 tablespoon olive oil
1/2 teaspoon cumin
1/2 cup mozzarella cheese
Salt and pepper to taste
Tortillas chips or Triscuits

Mix together the black-eyed peas, tomatoes, green onions, lime juice, cilantro, garlic, olive oil, cumin, mozzarella cheese, salt, and pepper. Chill for 4 hours. Serve as a dip with tortilla chips or Triscuits.

↷ Vegetable Dip ↶

1 cup mayonnaise
1 teaspoon tarragon or wine
   vinegar
Dash pepper
1/4 teaspoon salt

1/4 teaspoon curry
2 tablespoons chili sauce
1/8 teaspoon thyme
1/2 small onion, grated
Assorted vegetable pieces

Mix together the mayonnaise, tarragon or wine vinegar, pepper, salt, curry, chili sauce, thyme, and onion. Chill for one or two days before serving. Serve with celery, carrot sticks, radishes, cauliflower, zucchini, etc.

∽ Spicy Beef Dip ∽

1 pound ground chuck
½ cup finely chopped onion
Garlic powder
1 (8-ounce) can tomato sauce
¼ cup catsup
1 teaspoon oregano

1 teaspoon sugar
1 (8-ounce) package cream
  cheese, softened
⅓ cup Parmesan cheese
Crackers, chips, or party rye bread

Brown the ground chuck, onion, and garlic powder over low heat; drain. Add the tomato sauce, catsup, oregano, and sugar. Simmer for 30 minutes. Add the cream cheese and Parmesan cheese. Stir until melted. Serve hot in a chafing dish with crackers, chips, or party rye.

∽ Fish Mold Spread ∽

1 (10¾-ounce) can tomato soup
  (undiluted)
1 envelope unflavored gelatin
1 (8-ounce) package cream cheese
1 cup mayonnaise
½ cup celery, chopped fine

½ cup green pepper, chopped fine
¼ cup onion, chopped fine
Pimentos, cut fine
1 small can tuna or crab meat or
  salmon
Crackers

In a saucepan, mix together the tomato soup, gelatin, and cream cheese. Heat until warm. Remove from heat; let cool. Add the mayonnaise, celery, green pepper, onion, pimentos, and tuna, crab meat, or salmon. Serve with crackers.

ᗡ Layered Cheese Paté ᗡ

2 (8-ounce) packages cream
  cheese, softened
1¼ teaspoon dried Italian
  seasoning
⅛ teaspoon pepper
½ cup (2 ounces) shredded
  Gruyère cheese

¼ cup finely chopped pecans
¾ cup chopped fresh parsley
1 (3-ounce) package crumbled
  blue cheese
Fresh spinach leaves

Combine the cream cheese, Italian seasoning, and pepper;
mix until smooth. Line a lightly oiled 6-by-4-inch loaf pan
with plastic wrap, leaving a 2-inch overhang on each side.
Spread ⅓ of the cream cheese mixture in the loaf pan. Add the
Gruyère cheese. Sprinkle the chopped pecans over the cheese.
Top with ½ of the remaining cream cheese mixture. Add the
½ cup parsley. Sprinkle the crumbled blue cheese over the
parsley. Top with the remaining cream cheese. Press mixture
firmly into pan. Cover with overhanging plastic wrap. Chill
for 8 hours. Use the plastic wrap to lift the cheese loaf from
pan. Invert on spinach leaves. Remove plastic wrap and
serve at room temperature.

⤳ Rich and Creamy Coffee Punch ⤳

1 gallon strong hot coffee
1¼ cups sugar
2 cups whipping cream

1 pint vanilla ice cream, softened
1 pint chocolate ice cream, softened

Mix coffee and sugar, stirring until sugar dissolves. Chill well (overnight). Just before serving, fold in whipping cream and ice cream. Makes about 5 quarts.

⤳ Yellow Punch ⤳

3½ cups sugar
6 cups water
5 ripe bananas
2 (6-ounce) cans frozen orange juice concentrate

1 (6-ounce) can frozen lemonade concentrate
3 cans water
1 (48-ounce) can pineapple juice
3 quarts gingerale

Combine the sugar and 6 cups water. Bring to a boil; boil for 3 minutes. Remove from heat; let cool. Blend the bananas and 1 can orange juice concentrate in a blender. Combine the sugar water, banana mixture, remaining can orange juice concentrate, lemonade concentrate, 3 cans water, and pineapple juice. Freeze in ½-gallon containers. Thaw for 1½ hours before serving; mix in 3 quarts gingerale. Makes 50 servings.

◌ Strawberry Punch ◌

2 cups sugar
6 cups boiling water
2½ cups orange juice
½ cup lemon juice
4 cups unsweetened pineapple
    juice

2 (10-ounce) packages frozen
    strawberries with juice, thawed
1 (64-ounce) bottle lemon-lime
    carbonated beverage

In a Dutch oven, dissolve sugar in boiling water. Stir in orange juice, lemon juice, pineapple juice, and strawberries with juice. Pour mixture into a large plastic container. Freeze until firm. Remove from freezer 1 hour before serving. Place in a punch bowl; break frozen mixture into chunks. Add the lemon-lime beverage and stir until slushy. Makes about 6 quarts.

WCN Fruit Punch

2 quarts water
2 pounds sugar
2 sticks cinnamon
2 cups lemon juice
2 cups orange juice

2 (48-ounce) cans pineapple juice
4 quarts ginger ale
Orange slices, lemon slices, and
    maraschino cherries for garnish

Combine the water, sugar, and cinnamon sticks. Bring to a boil; boil for 10 minutes. Remove from heat; let cool. Add the lemon juice, orange juice, and pineapple juice. Pour some of the mixture into a ring mold. Add the orange slices, lemon slices, and cherries. Freeze. Chill the rest of the mixture. Add chilled ginger ale just before serving. Place the frozen ring in the punch bowl; add punch. Makes 100 servings.

∽ Hot Spiced Tea Mix ∾

5 cups Tang (dry powder)
2½ cups sugar
1¼ cups instant tea
2½ teaspoons ground cinnamon

1¼ teaspoons ground cloves
¼ cup lemonade mix (dry powder)

Mix together all ingredients. When ready to make tea, use 1 cup of the dry mix to 1 gallon boiling water. If desired, serve with a cinnamon stick in each cup.

∽ Iced Spiced Tea ∾

3 family-size tea bags
6 inches of mint
4 cups boiling water
½ cup lemon juice

1 cup sugar
2 cups boiling water
4 cups cold water

Combine the tea bags, mint, and 2 cups boiling water. In a separate container, combine the lemon juice, sugar, and remaining 2 cups boiling water. Let each mixture cool. Remove tea bags and mint leaves. Combine the two mixtures. Add the cold water. Serve over ice. Makes 8 (8-ounce) servings.

Soups
and
Salads

Frozen Fruit Salad

1 bottle maraschino cherries

1 can pineapple

1 can apricots

1 can white cherries

1 cup nuts

1 cup oil dressing

1 tablespoon gelatine with cup of cold

water

Set cup in hot water on stove and let

dissolve and beat into the dressing, then

beat 1 cup whipped cream into that. Put a

little sugar over fruit; drain fruit. Mix and

pack in ice and salt.

Mrs. J. W. Jakes

Recipe from WCN Cookbook of 1922

↶ Lentil Soup ↷

6 ounces green lentils
6 strips bacon
2 carrots
2 medium onions
2 stalks celery
1 (16-ounce) can diced Italian
  tomatoes and juice

2 cloves garlic, crushed
3 pints homemade stock or
  canned chicken broth
1 cup finely shredded cabbage
2 tablespoons chopped parsley
Salt and pepper to taste

Wash and drain lentils. Fry bacon and break into small pieces. Chop carrots into small pieces. Chop onions and celery. Stir the carrots, onions, and celery in a small amount of vegetable oil or bacon drippings. Toss vegetables for a few minutes on medium high heat, but do not brown. Stir in lentils, tomatoes, garlic, and stock. Bring to a boil and simmer gently, covered, for about 45 minutes. Stir in cabbage, salt, and pepper. Cook for 15 minutes more. Taste and adjust seasoning. Just before serving, stir in parsley.

↶ Spicy Tortilla Soup ↷

¼ cup chopped onion
1 clove garlic
1 teaspoon vegetable oil
2 zucchini squash, sliced or
  chopped
4 cups chicken broth
1 (16-ounce) can diced tomatoes,
  undrained

1 (12-ounce) can whole kernel
  corn, undrained
1 (15-ounce) can tomato sauce
1 tablespoon cumin (or more to
  taste)
Salt and pepper to taste
Tortilla chips
Cheddar cheese, shredded

Sauté the onion and garlic in the oil. Add remaining ingredients and bring to a boil. Reduce heat and simmer for 45 minutes. Serve in a bowl lined with tortilla chips. Sprinkle with cheese. *For a heartier soup, add 2 cups of chopped chicken.*

∽ Cabbage and Beef Soup ∾

1 pound ground chuck
½ teaspoon garlic salt
1 teaspoon garlic powder
¼ teaspoon pepper
2 stalks celery
1 onion, chopped

1 can hot chili beans
½ head cabbage, chopped
2 (14-ounce) cans Mexican-style
   tomatoes
2 cans water
4 beef bouillon cubes

Brown beef. Add remaining ingredients and bring to a boil. Reduce heat and simmer for 1 hour. *This soup keeps well in the freezer.*

∽ Vegetable Beef Soup ∾

1 quart water or chicken stock
   (or a combination of both)
1 large can V-8 juice
1 large can water
2 packages frozen mixed
   vegetables
1 large potato, chopped
1 large onion, chopped
1 (14½-ounce) can whole
   tomatoes, drained, cut in pieces
1 (12-ounce) can tomato paste
½ cup bite-size macaroni

¼ cup butter or margarine
Salt and pepper to taste
3 pounds lean ground beef
Any of the following according to
   taste: sugar, chopped parsley,
   chopped cabbage, chopped
   celery, chopped turnips,
   chopped rutabaga, rice, 1 can
   cream style corn, okra (cut up),
   barley, garlic, Worcestershire
   sauce, hot pepper sauce

Combine all ingredients except the ground beef. Bring to a boil and simmer on low for an hour. While mixture is simmering, brown the ground beef in a skillet. Drain and add to the vegetables. Simmer on low for about an hour. *To absorb grease, drop a leaf of lettuce in the soup while cooking. Discard the lettuce.*

∽ Cranberry Salad ∾

2 cups boiling water
1 (3-ounce) package orange-flavored gelatin
1 (3-ounce) package raspberry-flavored gelatin
1 (16-ounce) can whole cranberry sauce
1 (14-ounce) can crushed pineapple

Dissolve gelatin in 2 cups boiling water. Add the cranberry sauce and pineapple with juice. Mix well. Put into individual molds or a 9-by-9-inch dish. Chill until firm.

∽ Pink Arctic Freeze ∾

2 (3-ounce) packages cream cheese, softened
2 tablespoons sugar
2 tablespoons mayonnaise
1 can whole cranberry sauce
1 cup crushed pineapple, drained
1/2 cup chopped pecans
1 (8-ounce) carton whipped topping
Shredded lettuce

Cream the cream cheese and sugar. Stir in the mayonnaise. Fold in the cranberry sauce, pineapple, nuts, and whipped topping. Pour the mixture into a square container and freeze. Serve on shredded lettuce. Makes 10 to 12 servings.

⤫ Pineapple Lime Salad ⤬

1 (6-ounce) package lime-flavored
   gelatin
1 (8-ounce) can crushed
   pineapple

1 (9-ounce) carton whipped
   topping
2 cups buttermilk
1 cup chopped nuts (optional)

Combine gelatin and pineapple in a large saucepan. Heat just until gelatin is dissolved. Remove from heat and add the whipped topping. Stir until blended. Add the milk and nuts to the pineapple mixture. Pour into a 6-cup mold and chill until firm.

⤫ Layered Potato Salad ⤬

1½ cups mayonnaise
8 ounces sour cream
1½ teaspoons horseradish
1 teaspoon celery seed

1 teaspoon salt
8 potatoes, boiled
1 cup fresh parsley, chopped
2 green onions, chopped

Mix the mayonnaise, sour cream, horseradish, celery seed, and salt together in a bowl. Mix in potatoes. Top with parsley and green onions. Serve well chilled.

∾ Lime-Pear Salad ∾

1 can Bartlett pears
1 (3-ounce) package lime-flavored
  gelatin
1 (3-ounce) package cream
  cheese, softened

½ cup chopped pecans (optional)
1 (8-ounce) carton whipped
  topping

Drain pears, reserving juice. Add water to pear juice to make
1³/₄ cups. Pour into a small saucepan and heat to boiling.
Remove from heat. Dissolve gelatin in hot liquid. Let cool. Dice
pears. Combine cooled gelatin with softened cream cheese. Add
pears and pecans; mix well. Chill in a square glass dish till
slightly congealed. Remove from refrigerator. Fold in whipped
topping. Cover with aluminum foil and return to refrigerator.
Makes 9 squares.

∾ Orange Sherbet Gelatin Salad ∾

2 (11-ounce) cans Mandarin
  oranges
Orange juice

1 large package orange-flavored
  gelatin
1 pint orange sherbet

Drain the juice from the oranges into a 2-cup measuring cup;
add enough orange juice to make 2 cups. Heat in a saucepan
over medium heat. Add gelatin, stirring until dissolved.
Remove from heat. Add the orange sherbet and Mandarin
oranges. Pour into a mold or dish and chill until firm.

∞ Chicken and Fruit Salad ∞

2 cups cubed white meat of
  cooked chicken
1 orange, sectioned
¼ cup halved seedless grapes

¼ cup halved salted almonds
1 banana, sliced
¾ cup mayonnaise

Place chicken in a chilled bowl. Add remaining ingredients
and stir gently just until combined. Serve immediately.
Makes 8 servings.

∞ Party Chicken Pie Salad ∞

2 cups diced cooked chicken
2 cups diced celery
1 (9-ounce) can pineapple chunks,
  drained, juice reserved
1 (3-ounce) can English walnuts or
  pecans
1 small onion, finely chopped
1 cup sour cream

⅓ cup salad dressing
½ teaspoon salt
2 (9-inch) pastry crusts, baked and
  cooled
1½ cups grated sharp Cheddar
  cheese
Sliced green olives

Combine chicken, celery, pineapple, nuts, and onion. In
separate bowl combine sour cream, salad dressing, salt, and
¹/₄ to ¹/₂ cup of the reserved pineapple juice. Add half the
dressing mixture to the chicken mixture; refrigerate overnight.
To serve, fill pastry crusts with chicken salad mixture. Spread
with remaining dressing mixture. Garnish with cheese and
olives. *Serve with fresh fruit or congealed fruit salad for a great
luncheon menu.*

✂ Green Pea Salad ✂

1 can English peas	½ green pepper, chopped
2 stalks celery, chopped	¼ cup vegetable oil
1 bunch green onions, chopped	½ cup sugar
1 can shoe peg corn	½ cup vinegar

Combine the peas, celery, onions, corn, and green pepper in a large bowl. In a medium saucepan, bring the oil, sugar, and vinegar to a boil. Remove from heat and let cool. Pour cooled mixture over the vegetables. Toss and serve. Will keep well in the refrigerator for several days.

✂ Tomato Salad ✂

1 (16-ounce) can stewed tomatoes	3 drops hot pepper sauce
1 (3-ounce) package lemon-flavored gelatin	2 tablespoons lemon juice
	½ cup finely chopped celery
⅓ cup water	¼ cup finely chopped onion

Place tomatoes in a saucepan and bring to a boil, stirring to break the tomatoes up. Reduce heat to low. Add gelatin and stir until dissolved. Remove from heat. Add remaining ingredients. Chill until firm. Makes six servings. *Excellent with casseroles or quiche.*

✂ Tomato Aspic ✂

1 (3-ounce) package lemon-flavored gelatin	1 teaspoon Worcestershire sauce
	½ cup chopped celery
1 pint tomato or V-8 juice, heated	1 small green pepper, chopped
¼ teaspoon salt	½ cup diced cucumber
2 teaspoons lemon juice	1 tablespoon grated onion

Combine the gelatin and tomato juice. Add remaining ingredients and mix well. Pour into mold and chill.

WCN Molded Cucumber Aspic

9 envelopes unflavored gelatin
9 3/4 cups cold water
1/2 cup sugar
6 3/4 teaspoons salt
1 1/2 cups vinegar
5 1/2 cups peeled, seeded, and
 diced cucumber

3/4 cup finely chopped scallions
6 tablespoons finely chopped fresh
 parsley
1 medium cucumber

Mix the gelatin with 6 3/4 cups of the cold water. Heat slowly over low heat, stirring constantly until gelatin dissolves. Add the sugar and salt. Stir until dissolved. Add the remaining 3 cups cold water and vinegar to the gelatin mixture. Mix well. Pour 2 teaspoons of gelatin mixture into each of 20 individual molds. Chill until firm. To the remaining gelatin mixture add the diced cucumber, scallions, and parsley. Mix well. Let cool. Chill until thick and syrupy. Peel the whole cucumber and cut into 20 thin slices. Put 1 slice in each mold. Fill each mold with the cucumber-gelatin mixture. Chill until firm.
Makes 20 servings.

WCN Marinated Tomato Slices

1/4 cup chopped parsley
1/4 cup oil
2 tablespoons vinegar
2 teaspoons prepared mustard
1 teaspoon salt

1 teaspoon sugar
1/2 teaspoon pepper
1 clove garlic, minced
1 teaspoon basil
1 or 2 tomatoes, sliced

Combine all ingredients except the tomatoes. Place the tomato slices in a bowl. Pour the dressing over the tomato slices. Marinate for at least 20 minutes, or overnight if desired.

WCN Congealed Asparagus Salad

1 1/2 cups water
2 packages plain gelatin
1 cup sugar
1/2 cup vinegar
1/2 teaspoon salt
1 cup chopped celery
1/2 cup chopped pecans

2 tablespoons drained, chopped
  pimentos
2 teaspoons lemon juice
1 can asparagus spears, undrained
Lettuce and mayonnaise for
  garnish

Soak gelatin in 1/2 cup cold water. Heat to boiling the remaining cup of water with the sugar, vinegar, and salt. Add gelatin mixture to hot liquid, and stir until dissolved. Cool. Add celery, pecans, pimentos, lemon juice, and asparagus, including juice from the asparagus. Pour into an 11-by-7-inch dish and chill until set. Cut into squares. Garnish with lettuce and mayonnaise. Makes 10 to 12 servings.

☜ Marinated Tomatoes ☞

3 large tomatoes
1/2 cup olive oil
1/4 cup red wine vinegar
1 teaspoon salt
1/4 teaspoon pepper

Garlic powder
1 tablespoon parsley
2 tablespoons minced onion
1 teaspoon basil

Cut tomatoes into thick slices. Place in shallow dish. Combine remaining ingredients in a jar and shake well. Pour over sliced tomatoes. Refrigerate for several hours.

✑ Coke Salad ✑

2 cups boiling water
1 (3-ounce) package black-cherry-
flavored gelatin
1 (3-ounce) package lemon-
flavored gelatin

1 can black cherries, drained
1 small can crushed pineapple
6 ounces Coca Cola
1 cup pecans

Mix gelatin into 2 cups boiling water. Add remaining ingredients (and more water if necessary). Chill until firm.

✑ Coleslaw ✑

1 small head of cabbage, shredded
1 medium green pepper, chopped
1 small onion, chopped
½ cup vegetable oil
½ cup vinegar

1½ tablespoons mustard
2 packages sugar substitute
1 teaspoon salt
1 small jar pimentos
1 teaspoon celery seed (optional)

Combine cabbage, pepper, and onion in a mixing bowl. Set aside. Mix the oil, vinegar, mustard, sugar substitute, and salt together in a saucepan. Bring to a boil and remove from heat. Stir in the pimentos. Let cool. Pour cooled dressing over the salad mixture. Refrigerate for 3 hours. Add celery seed if desired. Makes 8 servings.

❧ Twenty-Four Hour Cole Slaw ❧

1 onion, shredded
3 or 4 carrots, shredded
1 head cabbage, shredded
¼ to ½ cup slivered red or green
   pepper (optional)
1 cup sugar

¾ cup vegetable oil
1 teaspoon dry mustard
1 teaspoon celery seed
1 cup vinegar
2 teaspoons salt

Toss together the onion, carrots, cabbage, and red or green pepper. Add the sugar; mix well. In a saucepan, combine the oil, mustard, celery seed, vinegar, and salt. Bring to a boil. Pour hot dressing over cabbage mixture. Mix lightly. Chill. Allow slaw to marinate for 24 hours. Stir well before serving. Makes 8 to 10 servings.

❧ Twenty-Four Hour Salad ❧

1 head of lettuce, shredded
¼ cup chopped onion
¼ cup chopped celery
1 cup frozen peas, uncooked
2 cups mayonnaise
1 tablespoon sugar

Grated Cheddar cheese
¾ pound bacon, cooked and
   crumbled
4 tomatoes, chopped
2 boiled eggs, sliced

Put the lettuce in a shallow 9-by-13-inch dish. Cover with the onion, celery, and peas. Spread with mayonnaise. Sprinkle with sugar and cheese. Cover with aluminum foil; chill overnight. Top with the bacon, tomatoes, and eggs. Makes 12 servings.

WCN Congealed Cabbage Slaw

1 small package lemon-flavored
  gelatin
1 cup hot water
¾ cup mayonnaise
¾ cup sour cream
½ teaspoon salt

1 tablespoon sugar
1 tablespoon vinegar
1 cup cold water
2 cups cabbage, chopped fine
2 tablespoons grated onion

Combine the gelatin and hot water, stirring until gelatin is dissolved. Add the mayonnaise, sour cream, salt, sugar, vinegar, and cold water. Combine gelatin mixture with the cabbage and onion. Chill until firm.

WCN Pea Salad

1 large can party peas
1 large can French-style green
  beans, drained
1 can pimentos, drained, chopped
  fine
4 stalks celery, chopped fine
1 large onion, chopped fine

1 large green pepper, chopped
  fine
¾ cup sugar
¼ cup hot water
½ cup vinegar
¼ cup oil

Mix together the peas, green beans, pimentos, celery, onion, and green pepper. In a saucepan combine the sugar, hot water, vinegar, and oil. Bring to a boil. Remove from heat and let cool. Pour cooled dressing over vegetables. Marinate overnight.

∽ Vegetable Salad ∾

¾ cup vinegar
¼ cup vegetable oil
1 teaspoon salt
¼ teaspoon pepper
1 tablespoon water
¾ cup sugar
1 (15-ounce) can small English
  peas, drained

1 (15-ounce) can French green
  beans, drained
1 (15-ounce) can shoe peg corn,
  drained
1 cup chopped onion
1 small jar pimentos
¼ cup chopped green pepper

Combine the vinegar, vegetable oil, salt, pepper, water, and
sugar. In a separate dish, combine the peas, green beans, corn,
onion, pimentos, and green pepper. Pour the liquid over the
vegetables. Marinate overnight in the refrigerator. Serve cold.
Makes 10 to 12 servings. *This is a good summertime salad.*

WCN Carrot Salad

4 cups shredded carrots
1 cup marshmallows
½ cup pineapple
½ cup raisins

¾ cup coconut
1¼ cups mayonnaise
1 cup whipped topping
¼ cup dried apricots, chopped

Combine the carrots, marshmallows, pineapple, raisins,
coconut, mayonnaise, and apricots. Fold in the whipped
topping. Chill.

WCN Spring Tonic Salad

1 (3-ounce) package lemon-
  flavored gelatin
1½ cups boiling water
1 cup cottage cheese
1 cup mayonnaise
1 medium carrot, grated

1 medium green pepper, chopped
1 cup celery, chopped
1 tablespoon chopped spring
  onions
Radish as desired for color
  (optional)

Dissolve the gelatin in the boiling water. Let cool. When gelatin is slightly set, add remaining ingredients. Chill until firm. Makes 10 to 12 servings.

WCN Tomato Soup Salad

1 can tomato soup
8 ounces cream cheese
2½ tablespoons lemon-flavored
  gelatin mix
½ cup cold water
1 cup mayonnaise

1½ cups chopped celery
1 medium green pepper
1 tablespoon grated onion
1 tablespoon Worcestershire sauce
1 cup mayonnaise

Combine soup and cheese in top of double boiler. Heat until cheese is melted smooth. Combine gelatin and cold water; let sit for 5 minutes. Add to soup mixture. Cool. Add remaining ingredients. Chill. Makes 8 to 10 servings.

WCN Three-Bean Salad

¼ cup chopped onion
1 can green beans, drained
1 can yellow wax beans, drained
1 can red kidney beans, drained
½ cup vegetable oil

½ cup vinegar
½ cup sugar
½ teaspoon salt
½ teaspoon pepper

Combine the onion, beans, yellow wax beans, and red kidney beans. Mix together the vegetable oil, vinegar, sugar, salt, and pepper. Toss vegetables and dressing lightly. Marinate for several hours. Serve salad well chilled.

✆ Mediterranean Pasta Salad ✆

1 can artichoke hearts, chopped
  into ½-inch pieces
1 can hearts of palm, chopped
  into ¼-inch pieces
1 can sliced black olives, drained
½ bag sundried tomatoes,
  rehydrated, drained, and
  chopped into ¼-inch pieces

Tricolor rotini pasta, cooked
  according to package directions
Tricolor bow-tie pasta, cooked
  according to package directions
½ bottle zesty Italian dressing
Feta cheese, crumbled

Mix together the artichoke hearts, hearts of palm, black olives, sundried tomatoes, and zesty Italian dressing. Place in container and chill. Place drained tricolor pastas in a separate container; chill. When ready to serve, combine the two mixtures and top with grated Feta cheese. *For a heartier dish, add diced cooked chicken breast.*

WCN Golden Glow Salad

1 (3-ounce) package lemon-flavored gelatin
1 cup boiling water
1 cup canned pineapple, diced or grated
1 cup pineapple juice (use juice from canned pineapple, adding water if necessary to make 1 cup)
1 tablespoon vinegar
1/4 teaspoon salt
1 cup grated carrots
1/2 cup diced crisp celery
1/2 cup pecans (optional)

Dissolve the gelatin in the boiling water. Let cool. Add remaining ingredients. Chill until firm.

❧ Frozen Cherry Salad ❧

1 (16-ounce) can cherry pie filling
1 (14-ounce) can crushed pineapple
1 (14-ounce) can sweetened condensed milk
1 (13-ounce) carton whipped topping
Salad Topping (optional)

Combine the pie filling, pineapple, sweetened condensed milk, and whipped topping; mix well. Freeze in a 9-by-13-inch dish. Cut into squares and top with Salad Topping if desired.

Salad Topping:

1 (4 1/2-ounce) carton whipped topping
1/4 cup instant orange drink mix
1/4 cup salad dressing (Miracle Whip)

Combine ingredients; mix well. Refrigerate until serving time.

WCN Orange Sherbet Salad

1 (6-ounce) package orange-
flavored gelatin
2 cups boiling water
1 pint orange sherbet

1 (11-ounce) can Mandarin
oranges
2 bananas, diced
1 small can crushed pineapple

Dissolve gelatin in boiling water; add sherbet. Stir until dissolved. Add remaining ingredients. Chill until firm.

WCN Curried Fruit

1 can peaches
1 can pears
1 small can pineapple

1/3 cup butter, melted
3/4 cup brown sugar
4 teaspoons curry powder

Preheat oven to 350 degrees. Place fruit in dish. Combine the butter, brown sugar, and curry powder. Pour over fruit. Bake for 1 hour. Cool and reheat for serving.

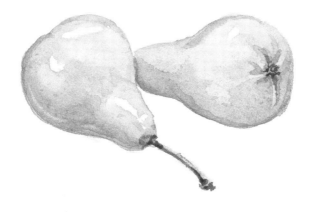

WCN Frozen Fruit Salad

2 egg yolks
2 tablespoons sugar
2 tablespoons vinegar
1 cup miniature marshmallows
3/4 cup mayonnaise

6 cups any chopped fruit, plus 1/2
 cup chopped maraschino
 cherries
1 1/2 cups whipped topping

In a saucepan, combine the egg yolks, sugar, and vinegar. Cook over medium heat until thick. Add the marshmallows. Remove from heat and let cool. Add the mayonnaise and fruit. Fold in the whipped topping. Freeze until firm.

WCN Buttermilk Salad

1 can crushed pineapple,
 undrained
1 (3-ounce) package apricot- or
 strawberry-flavored gelatin
2 cups buttermilk

1 (9-ounce) carton whipped
 topping
3/4 cup chopped nuts

Put the pineapple with juice in a saucepan. Bring to a boil. Add gelatin and stir until dissolved. Remove from heat and let cool. Add the buttermilk, whipped topping, and nuts. Refrigerate until firm.

⊙ Fruit Salad ⊙

1 can peach pie filling
1 can pineapple chunks, drained
1 can fruit cocktail, drained

1 pint frozen strawberries
3 bananas, sliced (optional)
1 can peaches, drained (optional)

Combine all ingredients. Chill.

WCN Fruit Cup

3 tablespoons Tang
2 or 3 bananas, sliced
1 package instant vanilla
  pudding mix
1 small can Mandarin oranges,
  drained, juice reserved

1 small can chunk pineapple,
  drained, juice reserved
Cherries as desired for color

Sprinkle Tang over sliced bananas until it is dissolved. Stir pudding mix into reserved fruit juice. Combine the bananas, oranges, pineapple, and cherries. Pour the pudding mixture over the fruit. Cover and chill.

∽ Mango Salad ∾

1 (29-ounce) can mangoes,
  juice reserved
3 cups liquid (mango juice
  plus water)
3 (3-ounce) packages lemon-
  flavored gelatin
1 (8-ounce) package fat-free
  cream cheese

Juice of 1 lime
Lettuce leaves
Fat-free sour cream to taste
Brown sugar to taste
Shredded coconut to taste

In a saucepan, combine the reserved mango juice and enough water to make 3 cups. Bring to a boil. Dissolve the gelatin in the boiling liquid; set aside. Put the drained mangoes and cream cheese into a blender and blend until creamy. Add to gelatin mixture. Stir in the lime juice. Pour into a ring mold, individual molds, or a 13-by-9-inch pan. Chill for 4 to 6 hours or overnight. Serve on bed of lettuce and top with your choice of sour cream, brown sugar, and/or coconut. Makes 12 servings. *This salad is good served with Mexican lasagna, chili, cheese, or rice.*

WCN Spiced Peach Salad

1 jar spiced peaches
1 small can pineapple
1 small can pears
1 (3-ounce) package peach-
  flavored gelatin

1 (6-ounce) package orange
  pineapple–flavored gelatin
$1/2$ cup pecan pieces

Drain enough juice from the peaches and pineapple to make a scant $3^{1}/2$ cups of liquid. Combine measured juice and gelatins in a saucepan. Heat and stir until the gelatin is dissolved. Cut peaches and pears into bite-size pieces. Add pineapple and nuts to peaches and pears. Combine fruit with gelatin mixture. Chill until firm.

WCN Five-Cup Salad

1 cup drained pineapple chunks
1 cup drained and halved
   Mandarin orange slices

1 can flaked coconut
1 cup miniature marshmallows
1 cup sour cream

Combine all ingredients. Chill well before serving.

WCN Peach Salad

1 small can crushed pineapple,
   drained, juice reserved
1 cup chopped canned peaches,
   drained, juice reserved
1 (3-ounce) package peach-
   flavored gelatin

1 envelope whipped topping mix
   (prepare as directed on package)
1 cup cottage cheese
10 maraschino cherries, chopped
1 cup miniature marshmallows
½ cup chopped nuts (optional)

Bring one cup of reserved juice to a boil; pour over peach gelatin, stirring until dissolved. Add 2 ice cubes; let cool. Stir in the prepared whipped topping; mix well. Add the cottage cheese, pineapple, peaches, cherries, marshmallows, and nuts. Mix well. Pour into a 9-by-9-inch glass dish. Chill until firm.

∞ Purple Lady Salad ∞

2 cups boiling water
1 (6-ounce) package black
  cherry–flavored gelatin
1 (16-ounce) can blueberries,
  drained
1 (16-ounce) can crushed
  pineapple, undrained

1 cup chopped pecans
1 (16-ounce) can fruit cocktail
1 (8-ounce) carton whipped
  topping

Dissolve the gelatin in the boiling water. Fold in the blueberries, pineapple, pecans, and fruit cocktail. Chill until almost congealed. Add whipped topping; mix well. Chill until firm.

∞ Cinnamon Applesauce Swirl Salad ∞

2 cups boiling water
1/3 cup cinnamon red heart
  candies
1 (6-ounce) package lemon-
  flavored gelatin
1 (1-pound) can applesauce

2 (3-ounce) packages cream
  cheese
1/4 cup cream
2 tablespoons mayonnaise
Lettuce leaves

Dissolve the candies and gelatin in the water. Stir in the applesauce. Blend until partially set. Pour into an 8-by-8-inch pan. Blend together the cream cheese, cream, and mayonnaise; stir gently into gelatin mixture for a swirled effect. Chill until firm. Cut into squares or use cookie cutters; serve on lettuce leaves.

Entrées

Veal Loaf

2 lbs. chopped veal

2 eggs

a teaspoon black pepper

1 teaspoon salt

1/2 pint water

10 cents worth of fat pork (chopped)

Mix all together; roll 1/2 dozen crackers;

take half and add to the other ingredients,

and the other half spread on top; before

putting in oven, dot the top with small pieces

of butter. Bake about 3/4 hour.

Mrs. W. H. Sory

Recipe from WCN Cookbook of 1922

❦ Beef Roast ❧

3- to 5-pound roast
1 package onion soup mix

1 can cream of mushroom soup
1 cup ginger ale

Preheat oven to 300 degrees. Put roast in covered pan. Add onion soup mix, cream of mushroom soup, and ginger ale. Bake for 3 hours.

❦ Beef Stew ❧

1½ pounds beef stew meat
1 large can V-8 juice
1 small can tomato paste
2 medium potatoes, chopped
1 package frozen green beans

1 medium onion, cut into small pieces
1 package frozen carrots
1 teaspoon basil (optional)
Salt to taste

Using a large pot, brown the stew meat. Stir in the V-8 juice and tomato paste. Add the potatoes, green beans, onion, carrots, and basil. Simmer for 45 minutes. Salt to taste. Serve with garlic toast. *Try freezing this stew in small containers to have on hand.*

❦ Chili ❧

1½ pounds ground beef
1 large yellow onion, chopped
½ green pepper, chopped
1 can tomato soup
1 can tomatoes
2 cans red beans

1 heaping tablespoon chili powder
1 scant tablespoon sugar
½ teaspoon Worcestershire sauce
3 small cloves of garlic
Salt and pepper to taste
Hot pepper sauce to taste

Brown beef. Cook the onion and pepper until soft. Combine all ingredients. Bring chili to a boil. Reduce heat. Simmer for at least one hour.

⚘ Spicy Texas Chili ⚘

1 small (3-pound) chuck roast
Water
2 tablespoons red wine vinegar
3 beef bouillon cubes
2 teaspoons chili powder
2 large onions, chopped
1 large green pepper, seeded and
   chopped
1 can chopped green chiles

Cayenne pepper to taste
   (about 1/2 teaspoon)
1 (28-ounce) can whole tomatoes
2 (16-ounce) cans black beans
Salt and pepper to taste
Cheddar cheese
Green onion
Tortilla chips

Trim excess fat from beef. Cut meat off bone in chunks. Put meat and bone into a heavy Dutch oven along with 1/2 cup water. Cover. Cook over medium-high heat until meat releases juices and turns gray, about 30 minutes. Uncover. Cook juices away. Turn meat until well browned on all sides. Lift out meat and set aside. To Dutch oven add 1/4 cup water and the vinegar. Scrape the pan to loosen browned bits. Add the bouillon cubes, chili powder, onions, green pepper, green chiles, and cayenne pepper. Cook, stirring, for 10 minutes. Add the tomatoes and their liquid. Break up tomatoes with a spoon. Add the black beans and their liquid. Return meat to the pan; stir to mix. Cover. Simmer until meat is tender enough to fall apart easily—about 2 hours. Discard bones. Skim off fat. Add salt and pepper to taste. Serve hot with Cheddar cheese, green onion, and tortilla chips.

∽ Beef Tomato Casserole ∾

1 pound ground chuck
1 (1½-ounce) package Sloppy Joe
  seasoning mix
1 cup water
1 (6-ounce) can tomato
  paste

2 (16-ounce) cans French-style
  green beans, drained and
  seasoned to taste
1 small jar sliced mushrooms,
  drained
1 cup grated Cheddar cheese

Preheat oven to 350 degrees. Brown beef in a large skillet.
Drain. Stir in the seasoning mix and water until mixture is
thickened. Add the tomato paste. Cover and simmer for 10
minutes. Add beans and mushrooms to beef mixture. Pour into
a 2-quart rectangular casserole dish. Sprinkle cheese on top (or
stir it into the casserole). Bake for 20 to 30 minutes or until
bubbly. Do not overcook. Makes 6 to 8 servings.

∽ Mitzi's Chili ∾

6 slices of bacon, fried and
  crumbled
1 pound summer sausage, sliced
  into 1-inch pieces and fried in
  bacon drippings
1 pound ground chuck, browned
  in bacon drippings
1 large onion, chopped
1 bell pepper, chopped
2 cloves garlic, minced

1 jalapeño pepper, diced
¼ cup Worcestershire sauce
1 cup Burgundy wine
1 teaspoon dry mustard
1 teaspoon celery seeds
2 teaspoons chili powder
3 cups Roma tomatoes, mashed
1 (15-ounce) can pinto beans
2 (15-ounce) cans kidney beans

Combine the cooked bacon, sausage, and ground chuck in a
soup pot. In a skillet sauté the onion, green pepper, garlic, and
jalapeño pepper, and add the Worcestershire sauce, wine, dry
mustard, celery seed, and chili powder. Simmer over low heat for
10 minutes. Add vegetable mixture to meat in soup pot. Stir in
the tomatoes, pinto beans, and kidney beans. Simmer 1 hour.

◌ Mexi-Corn Lasagna ◌

1 pound ground beef or turkey
1 (17-ounce) can whole kernel
   corn, drained
1 (15-ounce) can tomato sauce
1 cup picante sauce
1½ tablespoons chili powder
2 teaspoons ground cumin
1 (16-ounce) carton fat-free
   cottage cheese

2 eggs, slightly beaten
¼ cup grated Parmesan cheese
½ teaspoon oregano leaves,
   crushed
1 teaspoon garlic salt
12 corn tortillas
1 cup (4 ounces) shredded sharp
   Cheddar cheese

Preheat the oven to 375 degrees. In a skillet, brown the beef or turkey; drain. Add the corn, tomato sauce, picante sauce, chili powder, and cumin. Simmer, stirring frequently, for 5 minutes. Combine the cottage cheese, eggs, Parmesan cheese, oregano, and garlic salt; mix well. Arrange 6 tortillas on the bottom and up the sides of a lightly greased 13-by-9-inch baking dish, overlapping as necessary. Top with half the meat mixture. Spoon the cheese mixture over the meat. Arrange the remaining tortillas over the cheese, overlapping as necessary. Top with the remaining meat mixture. Bake for about 30 minutes or until hot and bubbly. Remove from oven; sprinkle with the Cheddar cheese. Let stand for 10 minutes before serving. Serve with additional picante sauce. Makes 8 servings.

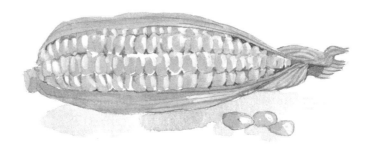

⤳ Beef Pimento with Horseradish Sauce ⤳

2 tablespoons margarine
2 pounds round steak, cut into
  1 1/2-inch cubes
1 (7-ounce) jar pimentos
1 large onion, sliced thin
1 teaspoon curry powder
1/2 teaspoon powdered ginger

1 teaspoon sugar
1 tablespoon Worcestershire sauce
Salt and pepper to taste
1 cup water
1 cup sour cream
2 tablespoons horseradish

Preheat oven to 300 degrees. Brown the steak in the hot margarine. Arrange in a medium casserole dish. Cut the pimentos into pieces (reserving one for garnish). Add pimentos and the liquid from pimento jar to the steak. Combine the onion, curry powder, ginger, sugar, Worcestershire sauce, salt, pepper, and water in the skillet. Bring to a boil; pour over the steak. Bake, covered, for 1 1/2 hours or until the steak is tender. Stir in the sour cream and horseradish. Garnish with pimento. *This is good served with fluffy hot rice and a green vegetable.*

☙ Holiday Beef Ribeye Roast ❧

2 cloves garlic, crushed	1 (4-pound) beef ribeye roast
1 teaspoon salt	Holiday Currant Sauce
1 teaspoon cracked black pepper	
1 teaspoon dried thyme leaves	

Preheat oven to 350 degrees. Combine the garlic, salt, pepper and thyme; press evenly into surface of roast. Place roast on a rack in a shallow roasting pan. Insert a meat thermometer so that bulb is centered in thickest part. Do not add water or cover. Cook for 18 to 22 minutes per pound of roast. Remove the roast from the oven when the meat thermometer registers 135 degrees for Rare or 155 degrees for Medium. Let stand for 15 minutes before carving. (The temperature will continue to rise to 140 degrees for Rare, 160 degrees for Medium.) Carve the roast into slices. Serve with Holiday Currant Sauce.
Makes 8 to 10 servings.

Holiday Currant Sauce:

1½ teaspoons dry mustard	1 (12-ounce) jar brown beef gravy
1 teaspoon water	¼ cup currant jelly

Dissolve the mustard in the water. Combine all ingredients in a small saucepan. Cook over medium heat for 5 minutes or until bubbly, stirring occasionally.

∽ Beef Burgundy ∾

2 pounds top round steak, cut into
   1-inch strips
4 tablespoons flour
Vegetable oil
1 medium onion, chopped
1 clove garlic, chopped
Water
Salt to taste
1 (8-ounce) container sour cream
1 (10-ounce) jar sliced mushrooms
Cooked egg noodles or rice

Coat the beef strips with flour. Cover the bottom of a Dutch oven with vegetable oil. Place the steak strips in the Dutch oven; brown. Add the onion and garlic. Cover with water and cook over medium heat until meat is tender, adding more water if needed. Salt to taste. Cool slightly. Add the sour cream and mushrooms. Heat. Form a nest of cooked egg noodles or rice on a platter. Fill the nest with the beef. *A good entrée to serve with a mixed vegetable casserole and a fruit salad.*

∽ Small Meatballs ∾

1½ pounds ground beef
1 pound ground veal
½ pound ground pork
3 cups bread crumbs
2 cups evaporated milk
1 cup chopped onions
2 eggs
1 teaspoon salt
½ teaspoon ginger
2 teaspoons butter
4 tablespoons flour
1 can bouillon soup
1 teaspoon instant coffee
Pinch salt

Mix together well the beef, veal, and pork. Combine the bread crumbs and milk, stirring till the milk is absorbed. Combine the meat mixture, bread crumbs, onions, eggs, salt, and ginger. Form into small balls. Brown in a Dutch oven in 2 teaspoons butter. Remove meatballs from pan. To the Dutch oven add the flour, bouillon soup, instant coffee, and salt. Stir until a gravy is formed. Add the meatballs. Simmer for about 30 minutes.

⌒ Dinner-in-a-Dish ⌒

4 tablespoons vegetable
   shortening
1 medium onion
2 green peppers, sliced
1 pound ground beef
1 teaspoon salt

¼ teaspoon pepper
2 eggs
2 cups fresh corn
4 medium tomatoes, sliced
½ cup dry bread crumbs
Margarine

Preheat oven to 350 degrees. Lightly cook the onion and green pepper in the shortening. Add the beef. Blend in the salt and pepper. Cook until beef is browned. Remove from heat. Stir in the eggs and mix well. Put 1 cup of the corn in the bottom of a baking dish. Layer half the meat mixture, half the tomato slices, the remaining 1 cup of corn, the remaining meat mixture, and the remaining tomatoes in the baking dish. Cover with the bread crumbs and dot with margarine. Bake for 30 minutes. *This Depression-era recipe from the 1930s is best made in the summer with fresh corn and fresh tomatoes.*

⌒ Favorite Meat Loaf ⌒

3 slices soft bread
1 cup milk
1 egg
1 pound ground beef
¼ pound ground pork
¼ pound ground veal

¼ cup minced onion
1¼ teaspoons salt
¼ teaspoon each of pepper, dry
   mustard, sage, celery salt, and
   garlic salt
1 teaspoon Worcestershire sauce

Preheat oven to 350 degrees. Tear bread into small pieces in a large mixing bowl. Add the milk and egg. Stir well. Add the beef, pork, veal, onion, salt, pepper, dry mustard, sage, celery salt, garlic salt, and Worcestershire sauce. Mix thoroughly. Form lightly into a loaf. Place in shallow baking pan. Bake for 1 hour. Makes 8 servings.

∞ Eggplant Casserole ∞

1 tablespoon butter
1 small onion, chopped
1 small green pepper, chopped
1 pound ground beef
4 small tomatoes, chopped or
   1 can whole tomatoes, chopped

1 large or 2 small eggplants,
   cooked until tender
1 to 2 cups bread crumbs
½ to 1 cup grated Cheddar cheese

Preheat oven to 350 degrees. Sauté the onion and green pepper in the butter until onion is clear. Brown the ground beef in a heavy saucepan or skillet. Drain. Combine all ingredients in a large skillet or saucepan. Simmer until tomatoes are cooked tender. Pour into a greased casserole dish. Top with the bread crumbs and Cheddar cheese. Cook for 20 to 30 minutes.

∞ Texas Hash ∞

1 pound ground beef
1 onion, chopped
1 small green pepper, chopped
1 small can mushrooms, liquid
   reserved

½ cup uncooked rice
1 teaspoon salt
1 teaspoon chili powder
1 can tomatoes

Brown the ground beef and onion in a skillet; pour off excess fat. Add the green pepper, mushrooms, mushroom liquid, rice, salt, chili powder, and tomatoes. Simmer for 20 to 30 minutes or until rice is tender.

∞ Johnny Mosetti ∞

2 tablespoons olive oil
5 garlic pods, minced
1 onion, chopped
1 cup chopped celery
1 cup chopped green and red
  peppers
2 pounds ground beef
1 (28-ounce) can roasted garlic
  tomatoes, diced
1 (6-ounce) can tomato paste

1 (8-ounce) can tomato sauce
1 (8-ounce) can mushrooms,
  sliced
½ cup green olives, sliced
1 tablespoon Worcestershire sauce
1 teaspoon salt
1 teaspoon pepper
2 cups grated Cheddar cheese
1 (10-ounce) package twisted
  macaroni

Sauté the garlic, onion, celery, and green and red peppers in the olive oil in a skillet. Remove sautéed vegetables from skillet. Brown the ground beef; drain. Add the sautéed vegetables. Add the tomatoes, tomato paste, tomato sauce, mushrooms, olives, Worcestershire sauce, salt, and pepper. Simmer for 30 minutes. Add 1 cup of the Cheddar cheese. Remove from heat. Preheat oven to 400 degrees. Cook the macaroni according to package directions; drain and stir into meat mixture. Pour into a greased 13-by-9-inch baking dish. Top with remaining cheese. Bake uncovered for 20 to 30 minutes. Makes 10 to 12 servings. *Serve this wonderful dish with French bread and a green salad when entertaining.*

∽ Saucy Manicotti ∾

1 box uncooked manicotti shells	3 cups bread stuffing
1/2 pound Italian sausage	20 ounces spinach, thawed and
1/2 pound ground beef	cooked
1 small onion	1/2 teaspoon garlic powder
1/2 box fresh sliced mushrooms	Salt and pepper to taste
2 eggs	1 (16-ounce) jar spaghetti sauce
1 cup shredded mozzarella cheese	White Sauce
1/2 cup grated Parmesan cheese	

Preheat oven to 350 degrees. Cook manicotti shells as directed on package. Drain and place on waxed paper. In a large skillet, brown the sausage, beef, onion, and mushrooms. Remove from skillet; drain on paper towel. In a large bowl, blend the eggs, mozzarella cheese, and Parmesan cheese until liquid. Add the sausage/beef mixture, bread stuffing, cooked spinach, garlic powder, salt, and pepper. Mix all ingredients well; fill manicotti shells with mixture. Pour half the spaghetti sauce into a 9-by-13-inch baking dish; spread evenly. Placed the stuffed shells side by side in dish. Prepare White Sauce and pour over stuffed shells. Pour remaining spaghetti sauce over the top. Bake for 35 to 40 minutes or until bubbly.

White Sauce:

3 tablespoons margarine	1/3 cup grated Parmesan cheese
3 tablespoons flour	Dash garlic powder
1 1/2 cups whipping cream	Dash nutmeg

Melt the margarine in a medium saucepan. Stir in the flour. Cook until smooth and bubbly, stirring constantly. Gradually stir in the whipping cream; cook until slightly thickened. While stirring, add the Parmesan cheese, garlic powder, and nutmeg. Blend well.

⌒ Barbecued Pork Chops ⌒

4 center-cut pork chops	½ teaspoon red pepper
2 large onions, sliced	1 teaspoon black pepper
2 tablespoons white vinegar	1 teaspoon paprika
1 tablespoon Worcestershire sauce	¾ cup catsup
1 tablespoon salt	¾ cup water

Preheat oven to 325 degrees. Place the pork chops in the bottom of a 9-by-9-by-1-inch baking dish. Cover with the sliced onions. Combine the vinegar, Worcestershire sauce, salt, red pepper, black pepper, and paprika in a measuring cup. Mix well and pour over the pork chops and onions. Pour the water and catsup over the pork chops and onions. Cover the dish with aluminum foil and bake for about one hour.

⌒ Sausage Casserole ⌒

2 pounds sausage	¾ teaspoon dry mustard
8 slices white bread, crusts removed	2¼ cups milk
	1 can cream of mushroom soup
12 to 14 ounces Cheddar cheese, shredded	½ soup can milk
	2 tablespoons butter
4 eggs	

Fry or microwave sausage; drain well. Arrange bread slices in a glass 9-by-12-inch baking dish. Cover with sausage and cheese. Beat eggs with the mustard and 2¼ cups milk; pour over the cheese. Refrigerate overnight. Let stand at room temperature for 1 hour. Preheat oven to 325 degrees. Dilute mushroom soup with ½ soup can of milk. Pour on top of casserole; dot with butter. Bake for 1 hour. Makes 8 servings.

❧ Betty's Ham Recipe ❧

8 to 10 slices ham, scraped,
boned, and trimmed

1 1/2 cups water
1/4 cup black coffee

Preheat oven to 350 degrees. Place ham slices on broiler pan rack, leaving a 1/2-inch space between each edge. Put water and coffee in bottom of broiler pan. Cover with heavy foil, crimping tightly around edges. Bake for 1 hour.

❧ Ham and Cheese Quiche ❧

1 cup milk
1/3 cup flour
4 whole eggs
2 cups shredded Cheddar cheese
1/4 cup finely chopped onion

1 1/2 cups diced ham
1/4 teaspoon caraway seed
Salt and pepper to taste
1 unbaked pie shell

Preheat oven to 350 degrees. Dissolve the flour in a small amount of the milk. Beat eggs. Combine all ingredients. Pour mixture into pie shell. Bake for 45 to 50 minutes. *Serve with a tomato salad.*

⬣ Quiche Lorraine ⬣

Dough for 1 pie crust
6 slices Canadian bacon
12 thin slices Swiss or Gruyère
    cheese, cut the same width as
    the Canadian bacon
4 eggs
1/2 teaspoon salt

1/4 teaspoon cayenne pepper
2 cups heavy cream
1 tablespoon flour
1 1/2 tablespoons melted butter
1 small can chopped pimentos
Grated Swiss cheese

Preheat oven to broil. Line a 9-inch pie plate with the pie crust dough. Broil the Canadian bacon. Drain on paper. Turn the oven down to 375 degrees. Cut the bacon slices into halves. Cover the pie crust bottom with half the bacon. Layer the cheese and remaining bacon so that there are two layers of each. Beat together the eggs, salt, cayenne pepper, cream, flour, and butter. Add the pimentos. Pour mixture over the Canadian bacon and cheese. Sprinkle with grated Swiss cheese. Bake for 35 minutes.

WCN Honey Pork Oriental

2 pounds pork shoulder steaks
2 tablespoons vegetable oil
1 envelope brown gravy mix
3/4 cup water
1/4 cup honey
3 tablespoons soy sauce
2 tablespoons vinegar

1 teaspoon ginger
1/2 teaspoon garlic salt
4 carrots, thinly sliced
1 medium onion, cut into wedges
1 green pepper, diced
Desired amount of cooked rice

Cut pork into squares. Brown in oil (about 15 minutes), stirring frequently. Combine the gravy mix, water, honey, soy sauce, vinegar, ginger, and garlic salt. Add to pork and cook for 20 minutes. Add the carrots; cook for 10 minutes. Add the onion and green pepper; cook for 5 to 10 minutes. Serve with rice.

WCN Sausage and Rice Casserole

1 pound sausage
1 onion, chopped
1 green pepper, chopped
1/2 cup chopped celery
2 cups cooked rice

1 (4-ounce) can pimentos
1 cup grated sharp Cheddar
  cheese
1 can cream of chicken soup
1 can golden mushroom soup

Preheat oven to 350 degrees. Brown the sausage (about 4 minutes); drain well. Combine sausage and remaining ingredients. Place in casserole dish. Bake for 45 minutes.

WCN Rice-Stuffed Ham Rolls with Mushroom Cheese Sauce

1/4 cup margarine
1 cup sliced mushrooms
1/4 cup all-purpose flour
1 cup chicken broth
1 cup half-and-half

1 cup shredded Cheddar cheese
1 cup wild rice
1 cup cooked, finely chopped
  chicken
8 ham slices

Preheat oven to 350 degrees. Melt the margarine in a skillet over low heat. Add the mushrooms and sauté. Add the flour, chicken broth, half-and-half, and Cheddar cheese. Cook until thickened. Remove from heat. Combine the rice and chicken. Place 1/4 cup of the rice-chicken mixture in the center of each ham slice; roll up slices. Place in a casserole dish. Spoon sauce over rolls. Bake for 15 to 20 minutes. Makes 8 rolls.

∽ Ribs and Kraut ∾

1 pound pork ribs (country style), salted and peppered	2 or 3 tart baking apples, cut in quarters
2 (16-ounce) cans sauerkraut	1 cup brown sugar

Preheat oven to 300 degrees. Place heavy aluminum foil in a roasting pan (or use a browning bag). Be sure to allow enough foil to fold over and seal tightly. Layer the sauerkraut and quartered apples in the foil. Sprinkle brown sugar over sauerkraut and apples. Add the seasoned ribs. Seal tightly and cook for 2 hours.

∽ Snowballs ∾

1½ pounds pork shoulder (ground)	1 cup rice (washed but not cooked)
Salt to taste	1 can tomato soup
Pepper to taste	2 cups water
Onion to taste	

Season the pork with the salt, pepper, and onion. Add the rice; mix well. Mold mixture into balls. Combine the tomato soup and water. Put the soup and pork/rice balls into a Dutch oven or large covered skillet. Simmer for 1½ hours. *Snowballs freeze well and are very versatile.*

∽ Crustless Quiche ∾

1½ cups grated cheese (1 part
   Swiss, 3 parts Cheddar)
½ cup chopped ham
1 jar mushrooms
3 eggs

1½ cups half-and-half
½ teaspoon salt
¼ teaspoon pepper
Dash of cayenne pepper
½ teaspoon powdered mustard

Preheat oven to 375 degrees. Layer the cheese, ham, and mushrooms in quiche pan or 8-by-8-inch pan. Beat together the eggs, half-and-half, salt, pepper, cayenne pepper, and mustard; pour over cheese, mushrooms, and ham. Bake for 45 minutes. Makes 6 servings. *To serve the leftovers, reheat the quiche at 300 degrees for 20 to 30 minutes.*

ᥫ Apricot-Glazed Pork Roast ᥫ

1 (2- to 3-pound) boned pork loin	1 teaspoon fresh grated ginger
⅓ cup apricot preserves	1 teaspoon dried thyme
1 tablespoon Dijon mustard	Salt and pepper to taste

Preheat oven to 325 degrees. Trim fat from roast. Sear in a roast pan. Combine the preserves, mustard, ginger, thyme, salt, and pepper. Brush over roast. Bake uncovered for 1 to 2 hours, basting 2 or more times during cooking. Remove from oven and let stand 15 minutes. Slice. In a saucepan, heat the remaining apricot mixture to boiling; cook for 2 minutes. Serve with the roast. Makes 6 servings.

WCN Spinach Quiche

6 slices bacon, cooked and crumbled, 1 or 2 teaspoons drippings reserved	2 cups grated cheese (Cheddar, Swiss, or mozzarella; a combination is good)
½ medium onion	2 tablespoons flour
4 eggs	1 (9-inch) unbaked pie shell
1 cup milk	
1 (10-ounce) package frozen spinach, cooked and drained	

Preheat oven to 350 degrees. Sauté the onion in bacon drippings. Beat the eggs and milk together. Add the onion, spinach, cheese, flour, and bacon. Mix well. Prick the pie shell and bake for 6 to 8 minutes. Pour mixture into pie shell. Bake for 1 hour.

⤳ Lamb Curry ⤵

2 tablespoons margarine
1¼ pounds lamb, cut in ½-inch
  cubes
¼ cup curry powder
1 clove garlic, minced
⅛ teaspoon thyme
1 can tomato soup, undiluted

½ cup water
½ cup chopped celery
¼ cup wheat germ
1 small eggplant, cubed
⅛ teaspoon salt
1 cup uncooked rice

Melt margarine in large pan on medium-high heat. Add lamb, curry powder, garlic, and thyme. Cook until lamb is brown. Add the soup, water, celery, and wheat germ. Cover and let simmer for two hours or until very tender. Add eggplant and salt; cook for 15 minutes longer. Prepare rice as directed on package. Serve lamb over rice. Makes 4 servings. *You may serve this dish with a variety of condiments: raisins, nuts, sliced ginger, cashews, coconut, roasted peanuts, etc.*

⤳ Lamb and Carrot Meatballs ⤵

1¼ pounds ground lamb
1½ cups finely shredded carrots
1 medium onion, finely chopped
5 dried apricots, finely chopped
1 egg or 2 egg whites

1 teaspoon salt
Dash of pepper
2 tablespoons cornstarch
1½ cups water
1 teaspoon basil

Combine the lamb, carrots, onion, apricots, egg, salt, and pepper. Shape into twelve medium or 24 small balls. Spray a large skillet with cooking spray; brown meatballs, turning to brown all sides. Pour off any accumulated fat. Blend the cornstarch and water; pour over meatballs, stirring gently until thickened. Add the basil. Cover and simmer for 25 to 30 minutes. Makes 4 to 6 servings.

◌ Chicken Teriyaki ◌

½ cup soy sauce
¼ cup brown sugar
1 clove garlic, chopped
1 tablespoon ginger

1 tablespoon vegetable oil
1 tablespoon sherry
2 pounds boneless, skinless
  chicken breasts

Combine the soy sauce, brown sugar, garlic, ginger, vegetable oil, and sherry. Add the chicken. Chill in refrigerator for 4 hours. Preheat oven to 325 degrees. Place chicken and liquid in a baking dish. Bake for 30 to 45 minutes until done. *This is also great on the grill.*

◌ Chicken and Saffron Rice ◌

2 (5-ounce) packages saffron rice
  (yellow)
2 cans cream of mushroom soup
1 (6-ounce) can sliced mushrooms
4 chicken breasts, cooked and cut
  into bite-size pieces

1 pound sausage, cooked and
  drained
½ cup milk
Cheese cracker crumbs
Melted butter

Preheat oven to 350 degrees. Cook rice as directed on package. Combine the rice, soup, milk, mushrooms, chicken, and sausage. Pour into a 9-by-13-inch casserole. Mix cheese cracker crumbs with melted butter; sprinkle crumb mixture over casserole. Bake for 35 minutes. Makes 8 to 10 servings.

☙ Buttered Chicken with Potatoes ❧

1 (4-pound) fryer or broiler,
   washed and cut into serving
   pieces
5 medium potatoes, quartered
Oregano

½ cup butter
1½ cups water
Salt and pepper
Juice of 1 lemon

Preheat oven to 350 degrees. Arrange the chicken in a small baking dish. Arrange potatoes around chicken. Sprinkle generously with oregano. Dab butter on potatoes and chicken. Add water, salt, and pepper to taste. Top with lemon juice. Bake for 60 minutes or until golden brown and tender. Baste occasionally with juice in pan. Serve hot. Makes 5 to 6 servings.

☙ Poppy Seed Chicken ❧

½ cup margarine
40 round buttery crackers
2 tablespoons poppy
   seeds

3 pounds chicken or 4 chicken
   breasts, cooked and boned
2 cans cream of chicken soup
8 ounces sour cream

Preheat oven to 350 degrees. Melt margarine. Crumble crackers into melted margarine. Add poppy seeds. Set aside. Chop cooked chicken; stir together with soup and sour cream. Stir in ¹/₂ of the cracker mixture. Pour into a 9-by-13-inch glass pan. Top with remaining cracker mixture. Bake for 30 minutes. Makes 8 servings. *Poppy Seed Chicken is a great luncheon dish.*

∽ Chicken Casserole ∽

2 cups diced cooked chicken
2 cans cream of chicken
  soup
1 cup sour cream

30 to 35 round buttery crackers,
  crumbled
1 teaspoon poppy seeds
1/2 cup margarine, melted

Preheat oven to 350 degrees. Spray a 9-by-13-inch casserole dish with cooking spray. Place chicken in dish. Combine the soup and sour cream; pour over chicken. Top with cracker crumbs and poppy seeds. Pour the margarine over the topping. Bake for 30 to 45 minutes or until bubbly.

∽ Chicken and Rice Casserole ∽

1 can cream of mushroom soup
1 can cream of celery soup
1 can cream of chicken soup
1 can water

1/2 cup margarine
1 cup uncooked rice
2 1/2 pounds chicken, cooked
Salt and pepper to taste

Preheat oven to 300 degrees. Combine soups, water, and margarine in a saucepan; bring to a boil. Remove from heat. Add the rice. Season chicken with salt and pepper; place in a 2-quart casserole dish. Pour soup mixture over chicken. Cover and bake for 2 hours. Makes 6 to 8 servings.

⌒ Hot Chicken Salad ⌒

2 pounds boneless chicken breast
Salt to taste
2 cups chopped celery, tops
 reserved
1 tablespoon chopped onion
1 cup chicken broth
1 cup chopped almonds

1 small jar pimentos
1 tablespoon lemon juice
½ cup mayonnaise
1 teaspoon black pepper
½ cup grated Cheddar cheese
1 cup crushed potato chips

Cook chicken in water with salt and celery tops to taste. Cook chopped celery and onion in the chicken broth until tender. Cut the chicken into large pieces; add the cooked celery mixture, almonds, pimentos, lemon juice, mayonnaise, and black pepper. Pour mixture into a large buttered casserole dish, adding more broth if it seems too thick. Sprinkle the cheese over the mixture. Sprinkle the potato chips over the cheese. Bake for 30 minutes (longer if mixture has been kept in the refrigerator).

⌒ Grilled Rosemary Chicken ⌒

8 chicken breast filets
1 clove garlic
1 teaspoon salt
½ teaspoon black pepper

2 tablespoons lemon juice
½ cup olive oil
1 teaspoon Dijon-style mustard
1 tablespoon rosemary

Place chicken breast filets between two sheets of plastic wrap and pound until quite flat. Combine remaining ingredients in a tight-lidded container large enough to hold the chicken breasts. Place chicken in marinade and refrigerate overnight. Grill chicken on a very hot grill for 4 minutes on each side, being careful not to overcook.

⌒ Chicken Almond Casserole ⌒

2 (5-ounce) cans cooked chicken
2 cans cream of chicken soup
2 cups diced celery
2 tablespoons dried onion flakes
1 package slivered toasted
   almonds
½ teaspoon salt

½ teaspoon white pepper
   (optional)
1 tablespoon lemon juice
6 hard-cooked eggs, sliced
1 cup mayonnaise
1 cup soda cracker crumbs
Potato chips for topping

Combine all ingredients except potato chips; stir to mix thoroughly. Refrigerate overnight. Preheat oven to 350 degrees. Bake casserole until bubbly. Top with potato chips and bake for 10 minutes longer. Serve hot.

∞ Chicken Monterey ∞

4 to 6 chicken breasts	16 large mushrooms, sliced
Salt and pepper	2 to 3 teaspoons flour
¼ cup flour	½ teaspoon celery salt
½ cup butter	1 cup chicken stock
¼ cup onion, chopped	½ cup white wine
1 clove garlic, minced	1½ cups Monterey Jack cheese

Preheat oven to 350 degrees. Skin and bone chicken; cut in half. Pound breasts between 2 sheets of waxed paper until thin. Sprinkle with salt and pepper. Dust with flour. Sauté chicken in 4 tablespoons of the butter until golden, about 2 or 3 minutes. Place on platter and keep warm. Melt remaining butter in same skillet; sauté the onion, garlic, and mushrooms. Stir in 2 to 3 teaspoons of flour. Remove from heat. Stir in the celery salt, chicken stock, and wine. Cook, stirring constantly, until bubbly and thickened. Add cheese, stirring to melt. Arrange breasts in casserole dish. Pour cheese sauce over chicken. Bake for 15 to 20 minutes or until warm.

81

ᘓ Luncheon Chicken Casserole ᘐ

8 chicken breasts, skin removed, cooked (steaming is best) and cubed
2 cans cream of celery soup
2 cups fresh chopped celery
2 medium jars pimentos, sliced
2 medium onions, chopped
2 cans French-style green beans, drained and washed
2 cups low-fat mayonnaise
2 cans water chestnuts, drained, washed, and sliced in halves
2 boxes Uncle Ben's long-grain wild rice
1/2 cup uncooked white rice
Salt and pepper to taste

Preheat oven to 350 degrees. Combine the wild rice with the white rice and prepare according to wild rice package directions. Combine all ingredients thoroughly. Pour into a shallow 2¹/2- or 3-quart casserole dish. Bake for 25 to 30 minutes. *This casserole can be frozen (do not cook before freezing).*

ᘓ Puff Top Turkey Sandwiches ᘐ

4 slices bread
1 package frozen broccoli or asparagus spears, cooked and drained
2 cups chopped cooked turkey
1/2 cup mayonnaise
1/2 cup shredded Cheddar cheese
1/4 cup chopped onion (or dried onion if raw onion is too strong for your taste)
1/4 cup diced pimentos
2 egg whites

Toast bread lightly. Top each slice with broccoli or asparagus and 1/2 cup turkey. Mix together the mayonnaise, cheese, onion, and pimentos. Beat egg whites until stiff peaks form. Fold into mayonnaise mixture. Top each sandwich with mayonnaise mixture, covering entire surface. Place 6 inches from broiler and broil for 4 minutes. Makes 4 servings. *This is a great way to use leftover turkey.*

WCN Hot Chicken Salad II

1 can cream of chicken soup
2 cups chopped cooked chicken
1 cup chopped celery
2 tablespoons chopped onion
1/2 cup almonds, chopped and
  blanched
1/2 cup mayonnaise

1/2 teaspoon salt
1/4 teaspoon pepper
1 tablespoon lemon juice
3 boiled eggs
1/2 cup cracker crumbs or potato
  chips

Preheat oven to 350 degrees. Combine all ingredients in a baking dish. Bake for 40 minutes. Yield: 6 to 8 servings.

∞ Chicken Enchilada Pie ∞

1 (3-pound) chicken, cooked and
  boned, one cup broth reserved
1 can cream of mushroom soup
1 can cream of chicken soup
1 (4-ounce) can chopped green
  chiles
1 teaspoon chili powder

4 teaspoons minced onion
1/8 teaspoon garlic powder
1/4 teaspoon black pepper
1/4 teaspoon hot pepper sauce
4 cups corn chips
8 ounces Cheddar cheese, grated

Preheat oven to 350 degrees. Combine the cream of mushroom soup, cream of chicken soup, green chiles, chili powder, onion, garlic powder, pepper, hot pepper sauce, and chicken broth. Blend well. Cover the bottom of a 3-quart casserole with two cups of the corn chips. Spread half the chicken over this layer. Spoon half the soup mixture over the chicken. Spread half the Cheddar cheese over the sauce. Repeat layering of chips, chicken, soup mixture, and cheese. Bake for 25 to 30 minutes.

∽ Chicken Tetrazzini ∾

1 pound sliced fresh mushrooms
1/2 cup plus 1 tablespoon
   margarine, melted
1/2 cup dry sherry
1 1/4 teaspoons salt
3/4 teaspoon ground white pepper
6 (4-ounce) skinned, boned
   chicken breast halves
1/2 cup chopped onion
1/2 teaspoon minced garlic

1/4 cup plus 2 tablespoons flour
2 1/2 cups half-and-half
1 1/2 cups canned ready-to-serve
   chicken broth
1 cup shredded Fontina cheese
3/4 cup freshly grated Parmesan
   cheese
1 (16-ounce) package linguine,
   uncooked
1/2 cup fine, dry bread crumbs

In a skillet, sauté the mushrooms for 5 minutes in 2 tablespoons of the margarine. Add the sherry; cook for 2 minutes or until sherry is reduced to 1/4 cup. Add 1/2 teaspoon of the salt and 1/4 teaspoon of the white pepper. Place the chicken in a saucepan; add water to cover. Bring to a boil; cover, reduce heat, and simmer for 20 minutes. Drain; let cool. Shred chicken. Cook the onion in 1/4 cup plus 2 tablespoons margarine in a saucepan over low heat for 15 minutes. Add the garlic; cook for 1 minute. Add the half-and-half and chicken broth. Add the flour, stirring until smooth. Cook for 1 minute, stirring constantly until thickened. Remove from heat; add the Fontina cheese, 1/2 cup Parmesan cheese, 1/2 teaspoon salt, and 1/4 pepper. Stir until cheeses melt. Preheat oven to 350 degrees. Cook linguine according to package directions; drain. Combine the mushroom mixture, chicken, cheese mixture, 1/4 teaspoon salt, and 1/4 teaspoon pepper. Stir in linguine. Spoon into a greased 9-by-13-inch dish. Combine the bread crumbs, remaining 1/4 cup Parmesan cheese, and remaining 1 tablespoon margarine; sprinkle over chicken mixture. Bake, uncovered, for 20 minutes. Makes 12 servings.

✑ Chicken Breasts with Wine Sauce ✑

4 to 6 chicken breasts
Butter to taste
Salt to taste
Pepper to taste

1 can mushroom soup
Dried onion to taste
3/4 cup cooking sherry or wine
Cooked rice

Preheat oven to 425 degrees. Peel skin off chicken breasts. Butter, salt, and pepper each breast. Put in baking dish; pour mushroom soup over the breasts, covering each one. Sprinkle dried onions over each. Pour wine over breasts. Cover with aluminum foil. Cook 1 hour or until chicken is golden brown and tender. Serve with rice.

✑ Herbed Chicken en Casserole ✑

3 large chicken breasts, halved
Salt and pepper to taste
1/4 cup butter
1 can cream of chicken soup
1 (5-ounce) can boiled sliced
   mushrooms, drained

2 tablespoons chopped green
   pepper
1/4 teaspoon crushed thyme
1 can water chestnuts, drained
3/4 cup sauterne

Preheat oven to 350 degrees. Season the chicken with salt and pepper. In a skillet, brown chicken slowly in the butter. Place in an 11^1/$_2$-by-7^1/$_2$-inch dish. Add the cream of chicken soup, mushrooms, green pepper, thyme, and water chestnuts to the chicken drippings in the skillet. Stir in the sauterne. Heat mixture to boiling. Pour over chicken. Cover with foil; bake for 25 minutes. Uncover and bake for 25 to 35 minutes longer.

❧ Oriental Chicken with Cheese Soufflé ❧

½ cup butter or margarine	2 cups chopped cooked chicken
½ cup flour	½ cup sautéed mushrooms
1 tablespoon salt	½ cup sliced almonds
1 cup evaporated milk	1 cup sliced water chestnuts
2 cups milk	¼ cup pimento strips
2 cups chicken broth	Cheese Soufflé

Melt the butter in a saucepan; add the flour and salt, and cook until bubbly. Add the evaporated milk, milk, and chicken broth. Stir until smooth. Cook over hot water for 30 minutes. If necessary, thicken sauce with additional flour. Stir in the chicken, mushrooms, almonds, water chestnuts, and pimento strips. Serve immediately over Cheese Soufflé.

Cheese Soufflé:

3 tablespoons margarine	1 teaspoon prepared mustard
¼ cup flour	2 drops Worcestershire sauce
1⅞ cups milk	1 cup grated American cheese
Dash cayenne pepper	6 eggs, separated
1 teaspoon salt	

Preheat oven to 300 degrees. In a saucepan, combine the margarine, flour, milk, cayenne pepper, salt, mustard, and Worcestershire sauce. Bring to a boil; cook for 1 minute. Remove from heat. Add the American cheese. Beat the egg yolks until thick; add to cheese mixture, stirring constantly. Beat the egg whites until stiff. Carefully fold the egg whites into the cheese mixture. Pour mixture into a buttered baking dish; fill dish to the top. Bake in a pan of hot water until set (about 1 hour). Remove soufflé from oven; cut into squares.

∞ Hot Brown ∞

2 tablespoons butter, melted
2 tablespoons flour
½ teaspoon salt
1 cup milk
1 cup shredded sharp cheddar
 cheese

4 slices toast, crust removed
4 slices cooked turkey or chicken
 breast
4 tomato slices, halved
4 slices cooked bacon, halved

Preheat oven to broil. In a saucepan, combine the butter and flour to make a paste. Add the salt, milk, and cheese. Cook over moderate heat until thick and creamy. Keep hot. Cut the toast into triangles. Place 4 triangles of toast on an oven-proof platter (use two platters to cook all 8 triangles at once). Cut each turkey or chicken slice into two triangles; place one triangle on each triangle of toast. Pour the hot cheese sauce over the meat. Place half a tomato slice over each triangle. Broil until the tomato is lightly cooked and the sauce bubbles. Garnish with bacon. Makes 2 servings.

᪥ Chicken à la King ᪥

6 tablespoons butter
⅛ green pepper, sliced thin
1 (4-ounce) jar of mushrooms,
   drained, liquid reserved
4 well-rounded tablespoons flour
½ teaspoon salt
1½ cups milk
1 small jar chopped pimentos,
   liquid reserved

3 cups diced cooked chicken, 1½
   cups broth reserved
3 egg yolks, beaten
1 teaspoon lemon juice
Paprika
2 tablespoons sherry

Sauté the green pepper and mushrooms in the butter. Add the flour, salt, and milk. Stir over low heat until smooth. Add the pimentos, pimento liquid, chicken, chicken broth, and mushroom liquid. Add the egg yolks. Simmer slowly until thick. Add the sherry and paprika just before serving. *This may be served in pastry shells or tarts or over corn bread.*

WCN Hot Turkey Hustle Up

4 cups cooked, chopped turkey
1 cup finely chopped celery
2 tablespoons lemon juice
4 hard-cooked eggs, sliced
½ cup blanched, slivered almonds
¼ cup chopped pimentos
½ cup mayonnaise
1 (10½-ounce) can condensed
   cream of mushroom soup

1 tablespoon salt
1 tablespoon onion flakes or
   1 medium onion, chopped
½ cup flour
½ teaspoon salt
½ cup sesame seed
½ cup grated American cheese
¼ cup melted butter

Preheat oven to 350 degrees. Combine the turkey, celery, lemon juice, eggs, almonds, pimentos, mayonnaise, soup, 1 tablespoon salt, and onion in the order listed. Pour into an 8-by-12-inch baking dish. Combine the flour, 1/2 teaspoon salt, sesame seed, American cheese, and melted butter. Mix thoroughly. Pour over turkey mixture. Bake for 30 to 35 minutes.

WCN Green Noodle Casserole

2 tablespoons butter
3 medium onions, chopped
2 cups celery, chopped
2 medium green peppers, chopped
3 cups chopped cooked turkey
1 (8-ounce) package green noodles, prepared according to package directions

1/2 can ripe olives, sliced
1/2 can green olives, sliced
2 jars pimentos, drained
2 cans mushrooms, drained and sliced
1 can cream of mushroom soup
8 ounces Cheddar cheese, grated

Preheat oven to 350 degrees. Sauté the onions, celery, and green peppers in the butter until soft. Combine with remaining ingredients. Bake for about 45 minutes. If desired, sprinkle more Cheddar cheese over the top.

∽ Turkey Divan ∾

2 (10-ounce) packages frozen broccoli, or 2 bunches fresh broccoli
2 to 3 cups cooked turkey (or chicken), diced or sliced
1 cup herb dressing mix
2 (10¾-ounce) cans cream of chicken soup

1 cup mayonnaise
1 teaspoon lemon juice
1/2 teaspoon curry powder
1/2 cup shredded sharp Cheddar cheese
1 cup crushed butter cracker crumbs
2 tablespoons margarine, melted

Preheat oven to 350 degrees. Place the turkey (or chicken) in a flat baking dish. Cover with the broccoli and herb dressing mix. Mix together the soup, mayonnaise, lemon juice, curry powder, and Cheddar cheese; pour over turkey and broccoli. Combine the cracker crumbs and melted margarine; sprinkle crumb mixture over casserole. Bake for 25 to 30 minutes.

⤷ Turkey Black Bean Chili ⤶

1 cup coarsely chopped onion
½ cup sliced celery
2 (16-ounce) cans no-salt black
  beans
1 (10-ounce) can tomatoes and
  green chiles, chopped, juice
  reserved

6 ounces turkey breast, cooked
  and diced
1 tablespoon chili seasoning mix
Sour cream for topping
1 red pepper, cut into strips
  (optional)

Coat a large saucepan with cooking spray. Place over medium-high heat until hot. Add the onion and celery; sauté until tender. Transfer to a blender. Drain the beans, reserving liquid. Add half the beans and all the bean liquid to blender. Process until smooth. Return mixture to the saucepan. Add the remaining beans, tomatoes with chiles, turkey breast, and chili seasoning mix. Cook over medium heat until heated through, stirring frequently, adding liquid from tomatoes and green chiles if necessary for desired consistency. Ladle into bowls. Top with a dollop of sour cream and garnish with strips of red peppers if desired. Makes 5 (1-cup) servings.

ᨡ Salmon Loaf ᨡ

1 (15-ounce) can salmon, drained
2 cups soft bread crumbs (about
  2¹/₂ slices)
2 tablespoons chopped green
  onions
1 tablespoon butter or margarine,
  melted

¹/₂ teaspoon salt
¹/₈ teaspoon pepper
¹/₂ cup milk
1 egg, slightly beaten

Preheat oven to 350 degrees. Flake salmon, discarding skin and bones. Combine salmon, bread crumbs, onion, butter, salt, and pepper in a bowl. Mix well. Combine milk and egg; add to salmon mixture and mix thoroughly. Shape into a loaf in a greased 3¹/₂-by-7¹/₂-by-2-inch pan. Bake for 35 to 40 minutes. Makes 3 to 4 servings.

ᨡ Classy Crab Meat Casserole ᨡ

1 cup cooked rice
1 (6¹/₂-ounce) can flaked crab
  meat, drained
¹/₃ cup diced carrots
¹/₄ cup grated Cheddar cheese

¹/₄ cup sliced green onions
¹/₄ cup sour cream
¹/₂ teaspoon salt
¹/₈ teaspoon pepper
Paprika to taste

Preheat oven to 350 degrees. Combine the rice, crab meat, carrots, cheese, green onions, sour cream, salt, and pepper. Turn into 1-quart casserole or 2 individual baking dishes. Dust with paprika. Cover and bake for 25 minutes or until hot. Makes 2 servings.

∞ Hot Crab Sandwich ∞

4 English muffins (split)	1 can crab meat or frozen crab
½ cup softened margarine	½ teaspoon mayonnaise
1 jar (5-ounce) Old English Cheddar cheese	½ teaspoon salt

Preheat oven to broil. Mix the margarine and cheese together.
Combine the crab meat, mayonnaise, and salt; spread over the
muffins. Top with cheese mixture. Broil until brown. Makes 4
servings. *Serve with a congealed tomato salad.*

∞ Shrimp Crab Meat Casserole ∞

½ pound cooked fresh (or frozen) thawed shrimp	½ green pepper, chopped
1 package crab meat	½ cup salad dressing
1 small jar pimentos, diced and drained	½ cup milk
1 can cream of mushroom soup	1½ cups small shell macaroni, cooked
1 small onion, chopped	2 cups (8 ounces) shredded Cheddar cheese

Preheat oven to 325 degrees. Combine the shrimp, crab meat,
pimentos, cream of mushroom soup, onion, pepper, salad
dressing, milk, macaroni, and 1½ cups of the Cheddar cheese.
Mix well. Pour into a 9-by-13-inch dish. Sprinkle the remaining
½ cup cheese over the top. Bake for 30 to 40 minutes. *This dish
can be frozen before baking.*

∽ Shrimp au Gratin Supreme ∾

1 pound shrimp
4 tablespoons melted butter
3 tablespoons chopped onion
1½ cups whole milk
¼ cup flour

½ teaspoon salt
¼ teaspoon dry mustard
Dash black pepper
1 cup grated Velveeta cheese
¼ cup dry bread crumbs

Preheat oven to 350 degrees. Cut shrimp into small pieces; simmer lightly in water until they are pink. Drain and set aside. While shrimp are cooling, put 3 tablespoons of the butter in a saucepan; add the onions and cook until they are clear. Gradually add the milk and heat. While milk is heating, mix together the flour, salt, dry mustard, and pepper. When milk is hot, slowly blend in flour mix. Stir constantly to avoid limping. When sauce has thickened, add all but ¼ cup of the Velveeta cheese. Cook until cheese has melted. Add shrimp. Simmer for 2 minutes. Pour into a greased casserole dish. Combine the remaining ¼ cup cheese, 1 tablespoon butter, and bread crumbs. Sprinkle on top of shrimp. Bake for 15 minutes.

∽ Salmon Loaf ∾

1 (16-ounce) can salmon, drained
1 cup fine bread crumbs
1 egg, beaten
1 can cream of mushroom soup
1 tablespoon lemon juice

½ cup mayonnaise
½ cup chopped fine onion
¼ cup green pepper, chopped fine
Salt and pepper to taste

Preheat oven to 350 degrees. Remove the bone and skin from salmon if necessary; flake. Combine all ingredients and blend thoroughly. Spread in a greased 5-by-9-inch loaf pan. Bake for 1 hour.

❧ Olsen's Shrimp and Egg Creole Casserole ❧

1 tablespoon butter
½ cup green pepper, chopped
½ cup onion, chopped
½ cup celery, chopped
½ pound fresh mushrooms, sliced
1 (16-ounce) can chopped tomatoes

2 tablespoons butter
2 tablespoons flour
1 cup milk
Hot pepper sauce
8 hard-cooked eggs, sliced
2 cups cleaned and cooked shrimp
¾ cup bread crumbs
2 tablespoons butter, melted

Preheat oven to 350 degrees. Sauté green pepper, onion, celery, and mushrooms in butter until tender. Add tomatoes and simmer 20 minutes. Combine the butter, flour, and milk in a saucepan to make a white sauce. Cook until thickened; add the salt, pepper, Worcestershire sauce, and hot pepper sauce to taste. Stir the sauce into the vegetable mixture. Add eggs and shrimp. Pour into greased casserole dish. Combine bread crumbs and melted butter. Cover the shrimp mixture with buttered bread crumbs. Bake until bubbly, about 30 minutes. Serves 8 to 10. *This is an excellent brunch meal.*

Vegetables
and
Side dishes

Carrots and Rice

Scrape carrots and cut into thin slices and boil until tender in water or stock. Cook the rice until tender, then drain it. Season both the carrots and rice rather highly with salt and pepper. Make a white sauce and place alternate layers of rice, sauce and carrots in a buttered dish; sprinkle a little parsley over the layer of carrots, put buttered crumbs on top of all and bake in a moderate oven about 20 minutes.

Mrs. R. F. Williams

Recipe from WCN Cookbook of 1922

∞ Swiss Broccoli ∞

1 (10-ounce) package frozen
  broccoli or 1 pound fresh
  broccoli, cooked and drained
1 tablespoon butter
½ teaspoon minced onion
1 tablespoon flour

½ teaspoon sugar
⅛ teaspoon pepper
1 cup sour cream
3 slices Swiss cheese, cut into
  strips
Paprika to taste

Preheat oven to 350 degrees. Place the broccoli in a shallow buttered baking dish. Melt the butter and sauté the onion; do not brown. Stir in the flour, sugar, salt, and pepper. Remove from heat; stir in the sour cream. Pour the sauce over the broccoli. Place the Swiss cheese slices on the broccoli. Sprinkle with paprika. Bake for 15 minutes.

∞ Good Quick Green Beans ∞

2 cans French-cut green beans,
  heated and drained
2 tablespoons horseradish
¾ cup mayonnaise

1 teaspoon Worcestershire sauce
1 teaspoon lemon juice
3 hard-cooked eggs, diced

Combine all ingredients. Pour into dish and serve.

∞ Bean Bundles ∞

2 cans whole green beans
Bacon slices, cut in half

1 small bottle French dressing

Arrange the green beans in bundles of 8. Wrap ½ slice bacon around each bundle. Place in a 9-by-13-inch dish. Pour French dressing over bundles. Cover and chill for 3 hours. Preheat oven to 350 degrees. Bake uncovered for 40 minutes. Serve with a slotted spoon.

⚮ Barbecued Green Beans ⚭

2 (16-ounce) cans green beans
1 large onion, diced
3 slices bacon, cut up

1/2 cup catsup
1/4 cup vinegar
1/2 cup sugar

Preheat oven to 325 degrees. Brown the bacon and onion in a skillet. Add the catsup, vinegar, and sugar. Simmer until slightly thick. Drain beans; put in a casserole dish. Pour bacon mixture over beans. Stir. Bake for about 1/2 hour or until bubbly.

⚮ Peas Vinaigrette ⚭

1/2 cup cooked peas
1 cup cubed American cheese

1/2 cup bottled Italian dressing
Salad greens

In a medium bowl, combine the peas, American cheese, and Italian dressing. Toss with a fork, mixing well. Refrigerate, covered, for several hours or overnight, stirring occasionally. Serve on salad greens. Makes 2 to 3 servings.

⚮ Quick Corn ⚭

2 packages frozen shoe peg corn
1 heaping tablespoon cornstarch
1 tablespoon sugar

1 small can evaporated milk
1/2 cup margarine
Salt and pepper to taste

Combine all ingredients. Cook in a skillet over medium heat for about 20 minutes. Makes 8 servings.

∽ Corn Casserole ∾

¾ cup milk
2 eggs
1 small green bell pepper,
    chopped

1 can cream-style corn
½ cup oil
1 package quick corn bread mix
1½ cups grated Cheddar cheese

Preheat oven to 350 degrees. Combine milk and eggs; beat slightly. Stir in the bell pepper. Add remaining ingredients and mix thoroughly. Spray a casserole dish with cooking spray. Pour corn mixture into the dish; bake for 40 minutes.

∽ Shoe Peg Corn Casserole ∾

1 (16-ounce) package frozen shoe
    peg corn
½ cup celery, chopped
½ cup onion, chopped
½ cup bell pepper, chopped
½ cup sour cream

1 can cream of asparagus soup
½ cup shredded Cheddar cheese
2 rolls round buttery crackers,
    crushed
¾ cup butter, melted
2 cups slivered almonds

Preheat oven to 350 degrees. Mix vegetables, sour cream, soup, and cheese. Pour into a 2-quart casserole dish. Pour the cracker crumbs on the vegetable mixture. Drizzle butter on the crackers; top with almonds. Bake for 40 to 45 minutes, until brown.

∽ Fried Eggplant ∾

1 small eggplant
1 egg, beaten
1 tablespoon water

Cracker crumbs
Salt to taste

Slice eggplant into 1/2-inch slices. Combine egg and water. Dip slices into egg mixture and roll in cracker crumbs. Fry in deep hot oil for 2 to 5 minutes, until golden brown. Add salt to taste. Makes 8 slices.

∽ Mamma's Corn Pudding ∾

7 ears small-grain white corn, cut
   off cob
1 tablespoon flour
2 eggs

3 tablespoons sugar
1 cup milk
Salt to taste (1 teaspoon)
⅓ stick butter, melted

Preheat oven to 375 degrees. Mix together the corn and flour. Beat together the eggs, sugar, and salt. Stir in the milk and corn mixture. Pour into a greased casserole dish. Pour the melted butter over the corn. Bake for 30 minutes or until set in center. Makes 6 to 7 servings.

∽ Sweet Potatoes ∾

3 cups cooked, mashed sweet
   potatoes
1 cup sugar
2 eggs
1 teaspoon vanilla

½ cup milk
½ cup margarine
⅓ cup flour
⅓ cup margarine
1 cup chopped pecans

Preheat oven to 350 degrees. Cream the sweet potatoes in a mixing bowl. Add the sugar, eggs, vanilla, milk, and ½ cup margarine; mix well with an electric mixer. Pour into a large casserole dish. Mix together the flour, margarine, and pecans. Pour over sweet potatoes. Bake for 30 minutes.
Makes 8 to 12 servings.

☙ Rich Sweet Potato Casserole ❧

3 cups mashed, cooked sweet
   potatoes
1/2 cup milk
1/2 cup butter
3/4 cup sugar
2 eggs, beaten

1 teaspoon vanilla
1/4 cup brown sugar
1/3 cup flour
1/2 cup butter
1 cup chopped pecans

Preheat oven to 350 degrees. Combine the sweet potatoes, milk, 1/2 cup butter, sugar, eggs, and vanilla. Place in a greased casserole dish. Combine the brown sugar, flour, 1/2 cup butter, and nuts. Sprinkle over sweet potatoes. Bake for 30 minutes. Makes 6 to 8 servings.

☙ Sweet Potatoes Caramel ❧

3 medium-large sweet potatoes,
   peeled and cubed
1/4 cup sugar
2 eggs, beaten
1/4 to 1/2 cup butter, melted
1/2 cup whole milk
1 teaspoon vanilla

1 1/2 teaspoons Frangelico liqueur
   (optional)
3/4 cup brown sugar
1/3 cup flour
1/3 cup butter or margarine,
   softened
1 cup pecan pieces

Place sweet potato cubes in a saucepan with water to cover and bring to a boil. Reduce heat; cover and simmer for 20 to 25 minutes or until potatoes are tender. Drain. Preheat oven to 325 degrees. In a large mixing bowl, either mash potatoes by hand or with an electric mixer. This should produce about 3 cups. Add the sugar, beaten eggs, 1/4 to 1/2 cup butter, milk, vanilla, and Frangelico. Blend until fluffy. Turn mixture into a lightly buttered 8- or 9-inch casserole dish. Mix together the brown sugar, flour, 1/3 cup butter, and pecans, working with a fork to blend the butter well. Sprinkle over the sweet potatoes. Bake for 30 to 35 minutes, or until sweet potatoes are cooked through and the topping has browned. Makes 8 servings.

⤚ Baked Acorn Squash ⤙

2 acorn squash
4 tablespoons brown sugar
4 tablespoons butter or margarine,
  softened

2 teaspoons grated orange rind
1 cup orange sections

Preheat oven to 350 degrees. Cut squashes in half and remove seeds. Place squash cut side down in a shallow baking pan. Add water to a depth of 1/4 inch. Bake for about 40 minutes. Combine the brown sugar, butter, and orange rind; mix thoroughly. Remove squash from oven and carefully turn halves. Fill squash centers with the butter mixture. Top with the orange sections. Bake for 20 minutes longer or until tender. Makes 4 servings.

⤚ Asparagus Casserole ⤙

1 can asparagus
Margarine
24 round buttery crackers,
  crushed

2 hard-cooked eggs, grated
1 cup grated Cheddar cheese
1 can cream of mushroom soup

Preheat oven to 350 degrees. Drain asparagus, reserving 1/2 the juice. Grease a casserole dish with margarine. Add layers of cracker crumbs, asparagus, grated eggs, and cheese. Repeat layers, reserving some of the cracker crumbs. Mix reserved asparagus juice with the mushroom soup and pour over top. Sprinkle with additional cracker crumbs. Dot with margarine. Bake for 30 minutes. Makes 6 servings.

WCN Asparagus Casserole II

1 can asparagus, drained
1 can green peas, drained
1 can mushroom soup
1 cup mayonnaise
1 cup grated sharp Cheddar
cheese
1 teaspoon salt
1/2 teaspoon pepper
1 medium onion, chopped
2 eggs, beaten
1/2 cup crushed cracker crumbs

Preheat oven to 350 degrees Arrange half the asparagus in a 2-quart casserole dish. Cover with the peas. Mix together the soup, mayonnaise, cheese, salt, pepper, onion, and eggs to make a sauce. Pour half the sauce over asparagus and peas. Add remaining asparagus. Top with remaining sauce. Sprinkle cracker crumbs on top. Bake for 30 minutes.

ᦸ Hoppin' John ᦸ

2 cups black-eyed peas
1/2 pound salt pork or bacon
1 teaspoon hot pepper sauce
1/2 teaspoon salt
2 tablespoons bacon drippings
2 medium onions, chopped
1 cup uncooked long-grain rice
1 1/2 cups boiling water

Cover peas with 6 cups water; soak overnight. Cook with salt pork, hot pepper sauce, and salt on low heat until barely tender; drain. Sauté onion in bacon drippings. Combine peas, onion, rice, and boiling water. Cover and simmer 20 minutes or until rice is cooked and water absorbed. *A New Year's tradition for health and good luck.*

∞ Squash Casserole ∞

3 pounds yellow squash
2 large carrots
2 onions
1 small jar diced pimentos
1 small can mushroom pieces

2 cans cream of chicken soup
1 cup sour cream
½ cup margarine, melted
1 package herb or corn bread
   stuffing

Preheat oven to 375 degrees. Slice the squash, carrots, and onions. Put in a saucepan; add the salt and pepper. Bring to a boil and cook until vegetables are barely tender. Drain well. Drain the pimentos and mushrooms. Add to the squash mixture. Add the cream of chicken soup and sour cream. Mix well. Toss together the margarine and stuffing. Place a layer of stuffing in the casserole dish. Pour the squash mixture over the stuffing. Top with the remaining stuffing. Bake for 45 minutes.

∞ Western Baked Beans ∞

½ pound sausage
10 slices bacon, diced
½ cup onion, chopped
⅓ cup brown sugar
¼ cup catsup
¼ cup barbecue sauce
2 tablespoons mustard

2 tablespoons molasses
¼ teaspoon salt
½ teaspoon pepper
1 (16-ounce) can kidney beans,
   drained
1 (32-ounce) can pork and beans

Preheat the oven to 350 degrees. Brown the sausage and bacon together; drain. Sauté the onion. Combine all ingredients and mix well. Pour into a 3-quart casserole dish. Bake for 1 hour. Makes 10 to 12 servings.

WCN Vegetable Medley

1 (32-ounce) package frozen
   mixed vegetables
1/2 cup chopped onion
1/2 cup chopped celery
1/2 teaspoon salt
1 cup mayonnaise

1 cup grated American cheese
1/2 cup saltine cracker crumbs
2 hard-cooked eggs, chopped
1/2 teaspoon sugar
Hot pepper sauce to taste

Preheat oven to 350 degrees. Combine all ingredients; pour into casserole dish. Bake for 30 minutes. Top with additional cracker crumbs if desired.

WCN Company Coming Squash Casserole

1 1/2 pounds yellow squash
1 teaspoon sugar
1/2 cup mayonnaise (not salad
   dressing)
1/2 cup minced onion
1/4 cup finely chopped green
   pepper (optional)

2 or 3 tablespoons bacon bits
1/2 cup chopped pecans
1 egg, slightly beaten
1/2 cup grated Cheddar cheese
Salt and pepper to taste
1/4 cup butter
Bread or cracker crumbs

Preheat oven to 350 degrees. Cook squash; drain and mash. Add the sugar, mayonnaise, onion, green pepper, bacon bits, pecans, egg, Cheddar cheese, salt, and pepper. Mix well. Brown the bread or cracker crumbs in the butter. Pour squash mixture into a casserole dish. Top with crumbs. Bake for 35 to 40 minutes.

❧ Beets ❧

¼ cup cider vinegar
½ cup brown sugar
½ (6-ounce) can frozen orange
   juice concentrate

½ (6-ounce) can water
1 tablespoon cornstarch
2 jars or cans baby beets, drained
1 tablespoon butter

In a saucepan, combine the vinegar, brown sugar, orange juice concentrate, and half the water. Bring to a boil over medium heat. Combine the cornstarch and remaining water to make a paste. Add the cornstarch paste to the orange juice mixture; stir until thick. Add the beets and butter. Heat thoroughly.

❧ Potato Casserole ❧

1 (2-pound) package frozen diced
   potatoes, thawed
1 can cream of chicken soup
1 (8-ounce) carton sour cream

1 (8-ounce) package shredded
   Cheddar cheese
1 small onion, diced

Preheat oven to 350 degrees. Combine all ingredients. Mix well. Bake, covered, for 1 hour. Remove cover and bake for 10 minutes.

∽ Stuffed Baked Potatoes ∽

6 baking potatoes
¼ cup butter or margarine,
  softened
1 (3-ounce) package cream
  cheese, softened

¼ cup Parmesan cheese
½ cup sour cream
Milk, if needed
Salt to taste
½ grated Cheddar cheese

Preheat oven to 400 degrees. Scrub and dry (and grease if desired) the potatoes. Bake for about 1¼ hours or until done. Remove from oven; do not turn oven off. Using oven mitts or potholders to prevent burning hands, immediately slice potatoes lengthwise about ¼ inch from top. Carefully scoop out the potato meat and put in a mixing bowl. Set potato shells aside. To the mixing bowl add the butter, cream cheese, Parmesan cheese, and sour cream. Cream thoroughly. Add a small amount of milk if mixture is too stiff. Add salt to taste. Fill potato shells with mixture; top with grated Cheddar cheese. Bake for 10 to 15 minutes. Makes 6 servings. *These potatoes freeze well. Prepare them early in the day or well in advance, then freeze. Thaw before heating.*

⤜ Marinated Mushrooms ⤝

1 pound medium mushrooms	Garlic powder
¾ bottle Italian dressing	Salt and pepper to taste
½ cup dry white wine	⅛ teaspoon tarragon leaves
1 tablespoon parsley flakes	(optional)
1 large onion, chopped	

Combine ingredients in a large saucepan. Bring to a boil and simmer for 3 to 5 minutes. Remove from heat and let cool. Refrigerate until chilled. Drain and serve.

⤜ Company Potatoes ⤝

8 to 10 medium potatoes	Salt and pepper to taste
1 (8-ounce) package cream cheese	Butter or margarine to taste
¼ cup or more sour cream	

Preheat oven to 325 degrees. Pare, boil, and drain potatoes. Mash; add cream cheese and sour cream. Beat until light and fluffy. Season to taste with salt and pepper. Spoon into 2-quart casserole. Top with butter or margarine. Bake for 20 minutes.

WCN Hash Brown Potato Casserole

2 pounds frozen hash brown
   potatoes, thawed
1/2 cup melted margarine
1/4 teaspoon pepper
1 teaspoon salt
1/2 cup chopped onion

1 pint sour cream
1 can cream of chicken soup
2 cups grated Cheddar cheese
2 cups crushed corn flakes
1/4 cup melted margarine

Preheat oven to 350 degrees. In a large bowl combine the potatoes, 1/2 cup melted margarine, pepper, salt, onion, sour cream, soup, and cheese. Combine the corn flakes and 1/4 cup melted margarine. Pour potato mixture into greased casserole dish. Top with corn flakes. Bake for 45 minutes.
Makes 12 servings.

∽ Veg-All Casserole ∾

2 cans mixed vegetables, drained
3/4 cup mayonnaise
1 cup sliced water chestnuts
1 cup chopped onion
8 ounces sharp Cheddar cheese,
   grated

1 roll round buttery crackers,
   crushed
1/4 cup margarine, melted

Preheat oven to 350 degrees. Combine the mixed vegetables, mayonnaise, water chestnuts, onion, and cheese. Pour into a buttered 9-by-13-inch baking dish. Mix together the crushed crackers and margarine. Spread cracker mixture evenly over casserole. Bake for about 30 minutes, or until bubbly.

∽ Granny's Okra and Tomatoes ∾

1 cup cut okra
¼ cup vegetable oil
1 medium onion, chopped
1 green pepper, chopped
1½ cups tomatoes, peeled and
   cut up

1 scant tablespoon sugar
1 teaspoon flour
½ teaspoon salt
Dash of pepper

Cook the okra in water for 10 minutes; drain. Sauté the onions and green pepper in the oil. Add the chopped tomatoes. Mix together the sugar, flour, salt, and pepper. Add to tomato mixture. Cook over low heat for 5 minutes. Add the okra and continue cooking until vegetables are tender but not mushy. Makes 4 servings.

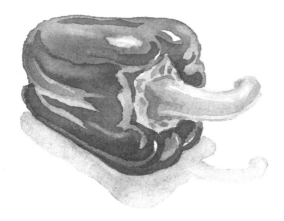

WCN Spinach Soufflé

2 eggs, separated
2 cups milk
2 cups chopped cooked spinach, well drained
1½ cups cracker crumbs

1 small onion, minced
1 small button garlic
Salt and pepper to taste
¾ cup margarine, melted

Preheat oven to 350 degrees. Combine the egg yolks and milk; mix well. Add the spinach, crumbs, onion, garlic, salt, and pepper. Add ½ the melted margarine. Beat the egg whites; fold into the spinach mixture. Put the remaining margarine in a casserole dish. Pour spinach mixture into dish. Cook in a pan of water for 45 minutes.

WCN Spinach Casserole

2 packages frozen chopped spinach
1 cup grated sharp Cheddar cheese
½ cup mayonnaise

1 can mushroom soup
½ cup chopped onion
Mushrooms to taste
Bread crumbs

Preheat oven to 325 degrees. Drain spinach; combine with the cheese, mayonnaise, soup, onion, and mushrooms. Pour into a casserole dish and top with bread crumbs. Bake for 45 minutes.

WCN Broccoli Casserole

1 can cream of mushroom soup, undiluted

16 ounces Velveeta cheese, grated

1 small grated onion, cooked soft in butter

2 packages frozen chopped broccoli, cooked

Several dashes of garlic powder

Preheat oven to 350 degrees. Stir soup and most of the cheese together, reserving some cheese for topping. Add onion, broccoli, and garlic. Place in oven-proof dish. Top with the remaining grated cheese. Bake for 30 minutes or until bubbly.

Mixed Vegetable Casserole

1 (1-ounce) package ranch dressing mix

2 tablespoons vegetable oil

1 (32-ounce) bag frozen mixed vegetables

Preheat oven to 375 degrees. In a large bowl, combine the ranch dressing mix and the oil. Add the frozen mixed vegetables and toss to coat. Pour into a casserole dish. Bake for 30 minutes, stirring every 10 minutes.

⊃ Broccoli Corn Bake ⊂

1 (10-ounce) package frozen
  chopped broccoli, thawed
1 (16-ounce) can cream-style corn
1 cup cracker crumbs
1 egg, beaten

2 tablespoons butter
1 tablespoon minced onion
1/2 teaspoon salt
Dash pepper
2 tablespoons melted butter

Preheat oven to 350 degrees. Combine the broccoli, corn, 1/2 cup of the cracker crumbs, egg, 2 tablespoons butter, onion, salt, and pepper. Mix well. Place in a 1 1/2-quart casserole. Blend the remaining 1/2 cup cracker crumbs and 2 tablespoons melted butter; sprinkle over broccoli mixture. Bake for 45 minutes. Makes 6 servings.

⊃ Cabbage Casserole ⊂

2 cups chopped celery
3 cups cabbage, torn into bite-
  size pieces

1 can cream of chicken soup
4 ounces Cheddar cheese, grated
Bread crumbs

Preheat oven to 350 degrees. Cook the celery and cabbage in a small amount of salted water until tender (about 10 minutes). Drain well and place in a casserole dish. Pour the soup over the cabbage and celery. Sprinkle with the cheese and top with bread crumbs. Bake for 30 minutes.

∞ Fried Onion Rings ∞

1½ cups flour
1 (12-ounce) can beer
¼ teaspoon salt

2 large Bermuda onions
Vegetable oil

Combine the flour, beer, and salt. Stir well. Cover and let stand at room temperature for 1¹/₂ to 2 hours. Peel onions; cut into ¹/₄-inch slices and separate into rings. Dip onion rings into beer mixture. Fry in deep hot oil until golden brown. Drain on paper towels and sprinkle with salt.

∞ Marinated Carrots ∞

2 cans carrots, drained
1 can tomato soup
½ cup sugar
½ cup vegetable oil
¾ cup vinegar
1 teaspoon Worcestershire sauce

1 green pepper, chopped
1 small onion, chopped
1 teaspoon prepared mustard
Salt and pepper to taste

Combine the soup, sugar, vegetable oil, vinegar, Worcestershire sauce, green pepper, onion, mustard, salt, and pepper. Mix well. Add the carrots; marinate overnight.

∞ Green Rice ∞

½ cup margarine
1 package chopped broccoli, cooked and drained
¼ cup onion, chopped
½ cup celery, chopped
1 small can sliced mushrooms
1 can sliced water chestnuts
1½ cups cooked rice
1 can cream of chicken soup
¼ cup pimento
2 cups diced, cooked chicken
1 small jar Cheez Whiz

Preheat oven to 350 degrees. Sauté broccoli, onion, and celery in the margarine. Combine all ingredients and place in a large casserole dish; or, if desired, place mixture in 2 smaller dishes and freeze one for later use. Bake for 30 minutes or until bubbly.

∞ Cheese Rice ∞

1 small package Mahatma yellow rice, cooked
½ cup sour cream
¼ cup butter
1 cup shredded Cheddar cheese

Preheat oven to 350 degrees. Combine all ingredients. Pour into a buttered casserole. Bake for 20 minutes or until heated through. Makes 6 to 8 servings. *This is a wonderful side dish— quick, easy, and delicious!*

⬿ Chili Cheese Rice ⬿

1½ cups uncooked rice
2 cups fat-free sour cream
Salt to taste
8 ounces Monterey Jack cheese, cubed

4 (4-ounce) cans chopped green chiles, drained
½ cup shredded Monterey Jack cheese
Butter

Cook rice. Preheat oven to 350 degrees. Combine with sour cream and season with salt. Arrange half the mixture in a buttered 2-quart casserole. Layer with cubed Monterey Jack cheese and chopped chiles. Top with remaining rice mixture. Sprinkle shredded cheese over the top. Dot with butter. Bake for 30 minutes. *This recipe can be prepared ahead, then refrigerated or frozen. If frozen, thaw for 1 hour, then bake.*

⬿ Louisiana-Style Red Beans and Rice ⬿

1 pound dried kidney beans
1 pound smoked sausage
1 cup chopped onions
1 stalk celery, chopped
2 cloves garlic, chopped

1 green pepper, chopped
1 teaspoon black pepper
¼ teaspoon cayenne pepper
Salt to taste
2 cups uncooked rice

Cover kidney beans with water ½ inch above level of beans. Cook beans for 45 minutes. Add sausage, onions, celery, garlic, green pepper, black pepper, and cayenne pepper. Cook slowly for 2 to 3 hours. Salt to taste. Prepare rice according to directions on package. Serve beans over rice. Makes 10 servings.

❧ Linguine with Tomatoes and ❧ Artichoke Hearts

2 tablespoons olive oil
1 medium onion, chopped
3 large garlic cloves, chopped
1 (16-ounce) can Italian plum tomatoes, chopped, juices reserved
2 teaspoons dried basil, crumbled

2 teaspoons dried oregano, crumbled
1 (14¾-ounce) jar marinated artichoke hearts
12 ounces linguine, freshly cooked
1½ cups grated Parmesan cheese
Salt and pepper to taste

Heat olive oil in a large heavy saucepan over medium heat. Add onion and garlic; sauté until tender, about 5 minutes. Add tomatoes, reserved juices, basil, and oregano; simmer until sauce thickens slightly, about 8 minutes, stirring occasionally. Add artichoke hearts and marinade to sauce; cook for two minutes. Add pasta and 1/2 cup of the Parmesan cheese to the sauce. Toss until sauce coats pasta and mixture is heated through, about 2 minutes. Season pasta to taste with salt and pepper. Transfer pasta to a large bowl. Serve with the remaining 1 cup Parmesan cheese. Makes 4 servings.

❧ Swiss Eggs ❧

6 eggs, slightly beaten
1 cup shredded Cheddar cheese
2 tablespoons melted butter
1/2 cup milk

1/4 teaspoon prepared mustard
1/2 teaspoon salt
Dash of pepper
Green onion tops (optional)

Preheat oven to 350 degrees. Combine all ingredients in a buttered 1¼-quart dish. Bake for 25 minutes.

❧ Stuffed Tomatoes with Lamb and Feta ❧

6 tomatoes
1/2 cup butter
1 medium onion, finely chopped
1/2 pound ground lamb or beef
1/2 cup uncooked rice

1 teaspoon minced mint
1 teaspoon minced dill
Salt and pepper to taste
1/4 pound Feta cheese
1/4 cup water

Preheat oven to 350 degrees. Slice tops off the tomatoes and reserve. Remove tomato pulp and seeds; reserve the pulp. Sauté the onions in the butter. Add the lamb; cook for 5 minutes. Add the rice, mint, dill, reserved tomato pulp, salt, and pepper. Stir to blend. Fill the tomatoes with mixture. Crumble the Feta cheese over the top. Replace tomato tops. Pour the water into a casserole dish; place the tomatoes in the water. Cover; bake for 30 minutes. Makes 8 servings.

❧ Macaroni and Cheese ❧

1 (7-ounce) package macaroni, cooked and drained
1/2 cup butter, cubed
1 (1-pound) box American cheese or 1 roll Kraft garlic cheese, cubed
1 1/2 tablespoons parsley, chopped

1 1/2 tablespoons pimento, chopped
1 1/2 tablespoons onion, grated
1 teaspoon salt
1/8 teaspoon pepper
2 eggs, slightly beaten
2 cups milk
Paprika to taste

Preheat oven to 350 degrees. Combine the macaroni, butter, cheese, parsley, pimento, onion, salt, pepper, eggs, and milk. Mix well. Pour into a buttered baking dish. Sprinkle with paprika. Bake, uncovered, for 50 minutes.

Grits Casserole

4 cups hot water
1 cup grits
1/4 teaspoon salt
2 eggs, beaten, plus milk to equal one cup
1 tablespoon garlic cheese

Preheat oven to 350 degrees. Combine all ingredients. Mix well and pour in a casserole dish. Bake for 30 to 45 minutes.

Pineapple Delight

3 eggs
2 tablespoons flour
Pinch of salt
1/2 cup sugar
1 (16-ounce) can crushed pineapple
3 or 4 slices white bread
1/4 cup butter, melted
Cinnamon to taste

Preheat oven to 350 degrees. Beat eggs; add flour, salt, sugar, and crushed pineapple. Pour into an ungreased casserole dish. Cover with bread slices. Pour butter over bread. Sprinkle with cinnamon. Bake for 25 minutes.

Dried Fruit Casserole

1 package dried apricots
1 package pitted bite-size prunes
1/2 package dried peaches, cut into small pieces
1 (15-ounce) can chunk pineapple with juice
1 1/2 cups water
1 can cherry pie filling

Preheat oven to 325 degrees. In large bowl, mix together all ingredients. Pour into a deep baking dish. Cover with foil and bake for about 1 hour. Uncover and bake for 30 minutes longer.

∽ Hot Fruit ∾

1 package pitted prunes, chopped
1 package dried apricots, chopped
1 can pineapple tidbits or chunks, drained
2 cans Mandarin orange sections, drained
1 can cherry pie filling

Preheat oven to 350 degrees. Combine ingredients. Pour into a casserole dish and bake for 45 minutes.

∽ Yummy Fruit Casserole ∾

12 almond or coconut macaroons, crumbled
1 (20-ounce) can chunk pineapple, drained
1 (20-ounce) can apricots, drained
1 (20-ounce) can peaches, drained
1 can pears, drained
1 bottle Maraschino cherries, drained
½ cup brown sugar
½ cup sherry

Preheat oven to 350 degrees. Grease a baking dish with vegetable shortening. Layer the macaroons and all the fruit except the cherries, beginning with a layer of macaroons. Cover with cherries. Sprinkle with brown sugar and sherry. Cook for about 30 minutes, until bubbly. *This dish goes well with almost any meat.*

Breads

Including Sweet Breads

Salt Rising Bread

1 cup sweetmilk	1 teaspoon sugar
1/2 cup cornmeal	1 teaspoon salt

Place on stove and stir until thickens. Next morning add 1/2 cup hot water. Stir in flour sufficient to make a thick batter. Set in warm water to rise.

Now take 3 cups of warm water, 2 tablespoons lard, 2 tablespoons sugar and 1 tablespoon salt. Add this to the yeast and enough flour to make a stiff dough. Knead well, and set to rise in well greased pan, and when light, bake about 45 minutes in a moderate oven.

Mrs. W. Anthony Grigg

Recipe from WCN Cookbook of 1922

ෙ Buttermilk Biscuits ෙ

4 cups self-rising flour

1 cup margarine

2 teaspoons baking powder

2 teaspoons sugar

1 cup buttermilk

Melted butter

Preheat oven to 450 degrees. Using a pastry blender or food processor, blend together the flour, margarine, baking powder, and sugar until mixture is the texture of meal. Add the buttermilk; mix until dough is formed. Knead, then roll dough approximately 1/2 inch thick. Cut out biscuits with a biscuit cutter. Bake for 12 to 15 minutes. Brush with melted butter. Makes approximately 28 biscuits. *The dry mix can be made ahead and stored in a closed container in the refrigerator; add buttermilk and make biscuits as needed.*

ෙ Jalapeño Corn Bread ෙ

1 cup self-rising cornmeal

1 tablespoon baking powder

1 small can cream-style corn

1/2 cup vegetable oil

1 cup sour cream

1 cup grated sharp Cheddar cheese

2 eggs, beaten

Chopped jalapeño peppers to taste

Preheat oven to 400 degrees. Combine all ingredients. Bake in an iron skillet or muffin tins until brown.

⊗ Hush Puppies ⊗

1 cup cornmeal	1 finely chopped onion
1/3 cup flour	1 egg
1 teaspoon salt	Milk
1/2 teaspoon red pepper	Hot fat

Combine all ingredients, using enough milk for batter to almost drop from spoon. Dip up a spoonful and nudge it out with your finger into the fat. When hush puppies come to the top they are done. *These are thoroughly enjoyed when served at fish fries.*

WCN Oatmeal Yeast Rolls

1 1/2 cups boiling water	1 egg, beaten
1/3 cup vegetable shortening	1 cake yeast, crumbled, or
1/3 cup firmly packed brown sugar	2 tablespoons dry yeast
1 teaspoon salt	3/4 cup nonfat dry milk
1 cup rolled oats	4 cups sifted all-purpose flour

Combine the boiling water, shortening, brown sugar, salt, and oats in a 5-quart bowl. Cool to lukewarm. Add egg and yeast; mix well. Sift dry milk with 2 cups of the flour. Add to oat mixture; beat until smooth. Add enough of the remaining flour to make soft dough. Turn onto floured surface. Knead until smooth and elastic. Place in greased bowl, turning to grease surface. Cover with waxed paper and towel. Let rise in warm place for 1 hour or until doubled in bulk. Punch down. Let rise for 10 minutes. Shape into 32 balls, each 1 1/2 inches in diameter. Place 1 inch apart in 2 well-greased 8-by-8-inch pans. Cover. Let rise for 1 hour or until doubled in bulk. Preheat oven to 375 degrees. Bake rolls until brown.

WCN Dilly Bread

2 packages yeast
½ cup lukewarm water
2 cups cottage cheese
2 tablespoons margarine
4 tablespoons sugar
2 tablespoons dried onion

4 teaspoons dill seed
2 teaspoons salt
½ teaspoon baking soda
2 eggs, beaten
5 cups sifted flour

Dissolve yeast in water. Set aside. Heat cottage cheese in saucepan to lukewarm. Add margarine. Stir well. Add sugar, onion, dill seed, salt, soda, and eggs. Mix well. Stir in yeast mixture. Slowly add flour. Stir to soft dough. Grease top. Cover and allow to rise until double in bulk. Punch down. Place in 2 greased loaf pans. Let rise again until double. Preheat oven to 350 degrees. Bake for about 30 to 40 minutes.

WCN Corn Muffins

2 eggs, beaten
½ cup oil
1 cup sour cream

1 small (8-ounce) can cream-style corn
1 cup self-rising cornmeal

Preheat oven to 425 degrees Combine the eggs, oil, sour cream, and corn. Stir in cornmeal. Mix well. Pour into tins and bake until golden brown.

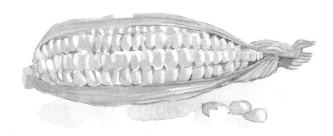

WCN Parker House Refrigerator Rolls

1 package dry yeast
1 cup warm water
   (105 to 115 degrees)
½ cup sugar
1½ teaspoons salt

⅓ cup vegetable shortening
1 cup water
2 eggs, beaten
6 cups all-purpose flour
Melted butter or margarine

Stir together the yeast and warm water. Combine the sugar, salt, shortening, and remaining 1 cup water in a small saucepan; heat, stirring often, until shortening melts. Cool mixture to 105 to 115 degrees. Combine yeast mixture, shortening mixture, and eggs in a large mixing bowl. Gradually stir in flour. Turn dough out onto a floured surface, and knead 5 to 8 minutes or until smooth and elastic. Place in a well-greased bowl, turning to grease top; cover and refrigerate for 1½ hours. Punch dough down; turn out onto a floured surface. Roll out to ¼-inch thickness. Cut into 2½-inch circles; brush with melted butter. Make a crease across each circle, and fold one half over. Gently press edges to seal. Place on greased cookie sheets and let rise in a warm place (85 degrees), free from drafts, for 1 hour or until doubled in bulk. Preheat oven to 400 degrees. Bake for 15 minutes or until golden brown. Brush rolls with melted butter. Makes about 3 dozen rolls.

WCN Broccoli Corn Bread

3/4 cup margarine
2 packages quick corn bread mix
4 eggs
1 medium onion, grated
1 package broccoli, chopped

1 (8-ounce) package cottage
  cheese
4 tablespoons sugar
1 cup flour

Preheat oven to 350 degrees. Melt margarine in pan. Mix together remaining ingredients; spread in pan. Bake until golden brown.

∽ Broccoli-Cheddar Corn Bread ∽

1 package quick corn bread mix
1 package frozen chopped
  broccoli, thawed
1 onion, chopped

1 cup shredded Cheddar cheese
3 eggs, beaten
1/2 cup margarine, melted

Preheat oven to 350 degrees. Combine all ingredients. Pour into a glass 2-quart casserole dish. Bake for 45 minutes or until brown.

WCN Egg Corn Bread

2 cups self-rising cornmeal	1¼ cups milk
1 teaspoon sugar	¼ cup melted vegetable
2 eggs, slightly beaten	shortening

Grease a baking pan and place in oven. Preheat oven to 450 degrees. Combine the cornmeal and sugar in a bowl. Set aside. Combine the eggs, milk, and melted shortening in a separate bowl. Add the cornmeal mixture. Blend thoroughly. Pour into hot pan. Bake for 15 to 20 minutes or until golden brown. *For buttermilk egg corn bread, substitute 1½ cups buttermilk for whole milk and add ¼ teaspoon baking soda.*

∽ Spoon Rolls ∾

1 package dry yeast	4 cups self-rising flour
2 cups warm water	¼ cup sugar
¾ cup vegetable oil	1 egg

Preheat oven to 400 degrees. In a mixing bowl, dissolve the yeast in the warm water. Add the remaining ingredients. Spoon into small greased muffin tins. Bake for 15 to 20 minutes. Makes 4 dozen small rolls. *This batter will keep for several days in the refrigerator.*

English Muffin Bread

6 cups unsifted flour
2 packages dry yeast
1 tablespoon sugar
2 teaspoons salt

¼ teaspoon baking soda
2 cups milk
½ cup water
Cornmeal

In a large bowl, combine 3 cups of the flour with the yeast, sugar, salt, and baking soda. Combine the milk and water in a saucepan; heat until very warm (120 to 130 degrees). Add to the flour mixture and beat well. Stir in the remaining 3 cups of flour to make a stiff batter. Divide in half. Put into two loaf pans which have been sprayed with cooking spray and dusted with cornmeal. Sprinkle more cornmeal on top of unbaked bread; cover. Let rise for 45 minutes. Preheat oven to 400 degrees. Bake for 25 minutes. Remove from pans immediately to cool.

Corn Bread

1 cup self-rising cornmeal
1 cup sour cream (regular or fat-free)

1 cup cream-style canned corn
½ cup vegetable oil
2 eggs

Mix above ingredients. Bake at 400 degrees for 30 minutes or until done.

⁓ Sour Cream Corn Bread ⁓

1 cup self-rising cornmeal
½ cup vegetable oil
1 (8-ounce) can cream-style corn

½ pint sour cream
2 eggs

Preheat oven to 450 degrees. Combine all ingredients. Fill a large skillet or three corn stick pans with batter. Bake for 25 minutes.

⁓ Mexican Corn Bread ⁓

1½ cup self-rising cornmeal
½ cup vegetable oil
Crushed red pepper to taste
1 cup buttermilk

1 cup shredded Cheddar cheese
1 can Mexi-corn, drained
2 eggs

Preheat oven to 350 degrees. Place all ingredients in a bowl and mix thoroughly. Bake for 30 to 35 minutes or until golden brown.

ᚘ Fancy Biscuits ᚘ

4 cups sifted flour
6 teaspoons baking powder
1 teaspoon salt

½ cup butter
2 eggs
1 cup milk

Preheat oven to 500 degrees. Sift together the flour, baking powder, and salt. Cut in the butter until the size of large peas (do not overmix). In a separate bowl, combine the eggs and milk. Add to the flour mixture, increasing the amount of milk if necessary to make a soft dough. Sprinkle a pastry cloth or dough board with flour and knead dough lightly. Roll about ¹/₂ inch thick and cut into desired shapes. Bake for 8 to 10 minutes or until lightly browned. Serve hot.

ᚘ Quick Biscuits ᚘ

1 cup self-rising flour
2 tablespoons mayonnaise

½ cup milk

Preheat oven to 375 degrees. Combine flour, mayonnaise, and milk in a bowl. Pour batter into a muffin pan. Bake for 10 minutes.

131

∽ Cheese Biscuits ∾

1 cup butter or margarine,
   softened
2 cups sifted flour
2 cups crispy rice cereal

1 (8-ounce) package sharp
   Cheddar cheese, grated, at room
   temperature
Salt and pepper to taste

Preheat oven to 400 degrees. Combine all ingredients. Mix well.
Roll into small balls; flatten with the bottom of a glass. Bake for
7 to 9 minutes.

∽ Nut Cheese Bread Sticks ∾

1/2 cup grated Cheddar cheese
1/2 teaspoon prepared mustard
1/4 cup mayonnaise
Dash hot pepper sauce

1/4 teaspoon salt
1/3 cup finely chopped pecans
5 thick slices enriched white
   bread

Combine the cheese, mustard, mayonnaise, hot pepper sauce,
salt, and pecans. Mix well. Remove the crusts from the bread;
toast bread lightly on both sides. Spread 2 tablespoons of the
cheese mixture on each slice of bread; cut each slice into 6 equal
strips. Toast under broiler, 5 or 6 inches from heat, for about
5 minutes. Makes 30 sticks. *Be sure not to use thin-sliced bread.*

⚭ Quick Coffee Cake ⚭

1½ cups sifted flour	2 tablespoons butter, melted
2 teaspoons baking powder	1 egg
½ teaspoon salt	½ cup milk
¼ teaspoon mace or nutmeg	Topping
6 tablespoons sugar	

Preheat oven to 425 degrees. Sift together the flour, baking powder, salt, mace or nutmeg, and sugar. Add the butter, egg, and milk. Stir to make a smooth batter. Turn into a shallow pan. Sprinkle Topping over batter. Bake for 25 minutes.

Topping:

4 tablespoons sugar	2 tablespoons flour
1 teaspoon butter	¼ teaspoon mace or cinnamon

Combine ingredients and mix with a fork.

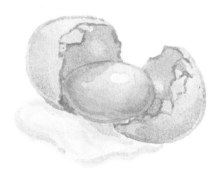

ᔆ Sour Cream Coffee Cake ᔆ

1 box yellow cake mix that calls
   for butter (but do not add
   butter; pudding mix is fine)
1 cup sour cream
1/2 cup sugar
4 eggs

3/4 cup vegetable oil
1 teaspoon vanilla
1 cup chopped pecans
3 to 5 tablespoons brown sugar
3 teaspoons cinnamon

Preheat oven to 350 degrees. Combine the cake mix, sour cream, sugar, eggs, oil, vanilla, and pecans. Beat just enough to remove lumps. Combine the brown sugar and cinnamon. Pour 1/2 the cake batter into a tube pan. Sprinkle batter with half the cinnamon mixture. Add remaining batter and sprinkle with remaining cinnamon mixture. Bake for 1 hour. Pierce with a toothpick to check for doneness.

ᔆ Strawberry Bread ᔆ

3 cups flour
2 cups sugar
1 teaspoon baking soda
1 teaspoon salt
1 teaspoon cinnamon

4 eggs, beaten
1 1/4 cups vegetable oil
2 (10-ounce) packages frozen
   strawberries, thawed and
   chopped

Preheat oven to 350 degrees. Combine the flour, sugar, baking soda, salt, and cinnamon in a large mixing bowl. Make a well in center of mixture. Combine the eggs, vegetable oil, and strawberries, stirring until well mixed. Pour strawberry mixture into the well in the center of the dry mixture. Stir until well combined. Grease and flour well two 9-by-5-by-3-inch loaf pans. Spoon batter into pans. Bake for 1 hour.

∽ Bran Muffins ∾

1 (15-ounce) box raisin bran
  cereal
3 cups sugar
5 cups flour
3 teaspoons baking soda
1 teaspoon salt
1½ teaspoons cinnamon

1 teaspoon allspice
1 teaspoon apple pie spice
1 teaspoon nutmeg
4 eggs
1 cup vegetable oil
1 quart buttermilk
1 to 2 cups raisins

Preheat oven to 400 degrees. Combine the raisin bran cereal, sugar, flour, baking soda, salt, cinnamon, allspice, apple pie spice, and nutmeg. Add the eggs, oil, and buttermilk. Mix well. Stir in the raisins. Pour batter into muffin tins; bake for 20 minutes. *Batter can be kept in the refrigerator for up to 6 weeks.*

∽ Strawberry Nut Bread ∾

1 cup margarine
1½ cups sugar
1 teaspoon vanilla
1 teaspoon lemon juice
4 eggs
3 cups sifted flour

1 teaspoon cream of tartar
1 teaspoon salt
1½ teaspoons baking soda
1 cup strawberry jam
½ cup sour cream
1 cup chopped nuts

Preheat oven to 350 degrees. Cream the margarine. Add the sugar, vanilla, and lemon juice. Beat until fluffy. Add the eggs one at a time, beating well after each addition. Sift together the flour, cream of tartar, salt, and baking soda. In a separate bowl, combine the jam and sour cream. Add the jam and flour mixtures alternately to the egg mixture. Beat until well combined. Stir in the nuts. Pour batter into 2 well-greased loaf pans. Bake for 50 to 55 minutes. Cool in pans for 10 minutes. Remove from pans and cool on wire racks. *This is a moist, delicious bread that keeps well. Jams other than strawberry can be used with equal success.*

135

⤜ All-Bran Muffins ⤛

2 cups boiling water
2 cups All-Bran cereal
5 cups sifted flour
5 teaspoons baking soda
2 teaspoons salt
2½ heaping cups sugar
1 quart buttermilk
1 cup vegetable shortening
  (heaping)

4 eggs
2 teaspoons orange flavoring
  (optional)
4 cups 40% bran flakes or other
  bran cereal
Dates, nuts, and/or raisins
  (optional)

Preheat oven to 425 degrees. Combine the boiling water and All-Bran cereal. Let cool. Combine the flour, baking soda, and salt. Add the shortening, buttermilk, eggs, orange flavoring, and bran flakes or other bran cereal. Add the cooled All-Bran mixture. Mix well. Stir in the dates, nuts, and/or raisins. Fill muffin cups ⅔ full with batter. Bake for 25 minutes. *This batter can be kept in a covered container in the refrigerator for about thirty days.*

136

WCN Plum Muffins

2½ cups self-rising flour
1 cup sugar
2 teaspoons allspice
3 eggs

1 cup oil
1 cup chopped walnuts
2 small (4-ounce) jars baby food plums

Preheat oven to 350 degrees. Mix together the flour, sugar, and allspice. In a separate bowl, beat eggs, oil, walnuts, and plums together. Add to dry ingredients. Bake for 15 minutes in miniature muffin tins.

WCN Sweet Potato Muffins

2 cups flour
2 teaspoons baking powder
½ teaspoon baking soda
1 teaspoon salt
1 teaspoon cinnamon
½ teaspoon cloves
1 egg

½ cup melted vegetable shortening
1 cup buttermilk
⅔ cup packed brown sugar
2 cups lightly packed shredded raw sweet potatoes

Preheat oven to 350 degrees. Combine flour, baking powder, baking soda, salt, cinnamon, and cloves. Beat together the egg, shortening, buttermilk, and brown sugar. Make a well in dry ingredients. Pour in liquid mixture and mix by hand just until ingredients are well moistened. Stir in shredded sweet potatoes. Bake in muffin tins for 20 minutes. Makes 18 muffins.

WCN Carrot Bread

3 cups all-purpose flour	3 eggs, beaten
1 teaspoon baking soda	1 cup vegetable oil
¼ teaspoon salt	2 cups grated carrot
2 cups sugar	1 (8-ounce) can crushed
1 teaspoon ground cinnamon	pineapple, drained
1 cup chopped pecans or walnuts	2 teaspoons vanilla

Preheat oven to 350 degrees. Combine the flour, baking soda, salt, sugar, and cinnamon. Stir in the nuts. Combine remaining ingredients; add to flour mixture, stirring just until dry ingredients are moistened. Spoon batter into 2 greased-and-floured loaf pans. Bake for 1 hour or until a wooden pick inserted in center comes out clean. Cool in pans 10 minutes, then remove from pans and let cool on wire racks.

WCN Lemon Poppy Seed Loaves

4 eggs, beaten
1 package lemon cake mix
1 (3-ounce) package instant lemon
  pudding mix
½ cup oil

⅛ cup poppy seeds
1 cup water
½ cup lemon juice
2 tablespoons sugar

Preheat oven to 350 degrees. Combine the eggs, cake mix, pudding mix, oil, poppy seeds, and water. Pour batter into 2 greased medium loaf pans. Bake for about 55 minutes. Combine lemon juice and sugar in a small saucepan. Heat until sugar is dissolved. Remove from heat; drizzle glaze over the baked loaves.

∽ Poppy Seed Bread ∽

3 cups flour
1½ teaspoons baking powder
1¼ cups sugar
1½ tablespoons poppy seeds
3 eggs
1½ cups vegetable oil

1½ cups milk
1½ teaspoons almond extract
1½ teaspoons butter extract
1½ teaspoons vanilla
Glaze

Preheat oven to 350 degrees. Combine flour, baking powder, sugar, poppy seeds, eggs, oil, milk, almond extract, butter extract, and vanilla in a bowl. Beat for 1 to 2 minutes. Do not overbeat. Pour into 2 greased-and-floured loaf pans. Bake for 1 hour. Let cool slightly. Spoon Glaze over warm loaves.

Glaze:

½ cup orange juice
¾ cup powdered sugar
½ teaspoon almond extract

½ teaspoon butter extract
½ teaspoon vanilla

Combine orange juice, powdered sugar, almond extract, butter extract and vanilla in a bowl. Stir until smooth.

∽ Pumpkin Muffins ∾

1 (2-cup) can pumpkin
1 can applesauce
2/3 cup water
1/4 cup honey
3 egg whites
1 1/2 cups whole wheat flour

1 1/2 cups white flour
1 1/2 cups wheat germ
1 1/2 teaspoons cinnamon
1 1/2 teaspoons nutmeg
1 teaspoon cloves
1 2/3 cups sugar

Preheat oven to 350 degrees. Mix the pumpkin, applesauce, water, honey, and egg whites. In a separate bowl, combine the whole wheat flour, white flour, wheat germ, cinnamon, nutmeg, cloves, and sugar. Add to the pumpkin mixture, stirring by hand to mix. Pour into muffin tins or 2 loaf pans. Bake regular-sized muffins for 20 to 25 minutes, small muffins for 15 to 20 minutes, and loaves for about 40 minutes. Makes 24 regular muffins, 48 small muffins, or 2 loaves.

WCN Ruth's Pumpkin Bread

3 cups sugar
4 eggs
1 cup vegetable oil
1 1/2 teaspoons salt
1 teaspoon cinnamon
1 teaspoon nutmeg

1 cup broken pecans
1 cup water
2 cups pumpkin
3 cups all-purpose flour
2 teaspoons baking soda
1/2 teaspoon baking powder

Preheat oven to 350 degrees. Mix ingredients in order given. Pour into 2 greased-and-floured loaf pans. Bake for 1 to 1 1/2 hours or until done.

❧ Pumpkin Bread ❧

3½ cups flour	2 cups pumpkin
1½ cups raisins	1½ teaspoons salt
3 cups sugar	2 teaspoons baking soda
4 eggs	1 teaspoon nutmeg
1 cup vegetable oil	1 teaspoon cinnamon
⅔ cup water	Pecans (optional)

Preheat oven to 350 degrees. Combine raisins and flour until raisins are thoroughly coated. Add remaining ingredients and mix well. Pour into a greased-and-floured stew pan, or use loaf pans (2 large, 4 medium, or 8 small). Bake for 1 hour (check after 50 minutes).

WCN Banana Nut Bread

¾ cup vegetable shortening	1 teaspoon baking powder
2¼ cups sugar	3 cups flour
3 eggs	¾ teaspoons salt
½ teaspoon vanilla	3 large ripe bananas, mashed well
⅓ cup buttermilk	1 cup chopped pecans or walnuts
1 teaspoon baking soda	

Preheat oven to 350 degrees. Cream the shortening and sugar. Add the eggs and vanilla; mix well. Dissolve the baking soda in the buttermilk. Sift the baking powder with the flour and salt. Add the flour and buttermilk alternately to the shortening mixture. Fold in the bananas and nuts. Spray two 9-by-5-inch loaf pans with non-stick cooking spray. Pour batter into pans; bake for 1 hour. Test for doneness with a toothpick. *This bread freezes well.*

WCN Zucchini Muffins

1½ cups all-purpose flour
½ cup sugar
1 teaspoon baking powder
½ teaspoon salt
½ teaspoon cinnamon
1 cup grated zucchini

½ cup chopped walnuts
½ cup raisins
1 egg
⅓ cup vegetable oil
¼ cup milk

Preheat oven to 400 degrees. Combine flour, sugar, baking powder, salt, and cinnamon in medium bowl. Mix in remaining ingredients all at once until just moistened. Fill 12 greased muffin cups ²/₃ full. Bake for 25 to 30 minutes, or until tops spring back when touched lightly with finger.

Desserts

Jam Pudding

3 eggs (beaten separately)

2 cups flour

1/2 cup butter

1 cup sugar

3 tablespoons buttermilk

1/2 teaspoon soda

1 teaspoon cinnamon, nutmeg and

    spice to taste

1 cup jam

Mix as you would cake. Serve with wine
or cream sauce.

Mrs. J. W. Black

Recipe from WCN Cookbook of 1922

∽ Carrot Cake ∾

4 eggs, well beaten	2 teaspoons baking soda
1½ cups vegetable oil	2 teaspoons cinnamon
2 cups flour	1 cup walnuts
2 cups sugar	1 cup crushed pineapple
Pinch of salt	Cream Cheese Frosting
3 cups grated carrots	

Preheat oven to 350 degrees. Combine eggs and oil. Add remaining ingredients one at a time; mix. Grease and flour two 9-inch cake pans. Pour mixture into pans; bake for 40 to 45 minutes. Use a toothpick to test for doneness. Remove layers from pans and cool thoroughly. Frost cake with Cream Cheese Frosting. Keep refrigerated.

Cream Cheese Frosting:

8 ounces cream cheese	¾ box powdered sugar
½ cup butter or margarine	1 teaspoon vanilla

Blend cream cheese, butter, powdered sugar, and vanilla until very smooth.

∽ Butter Cake ∾

1 box butter cake mix	1 cup sugar
¾ cup butter, melted	1 tablespoon vanilla
½ cup water	1 tablespoon butter flavoring

Prepare and bake cake mix according to package directions in a glass 9-by-13-inch pan. Combine the butter, water, and sugar in a medium saucepan. Bring to a boil; boil for 3 minutes. Remove from heat, and let cool. Add the vanilla and butter flavoring. Punch holes in the cake with toothpicks. Pour the icing over the cake.

◌ World Famous Peach Cake ◌

2 cups sugar
2 cups self-rising flour
1 teaspoon baking soda
1 teaspoon cinnamon
2 eggs

1 large can peaches, drained and
 sliced
½ cup butter, melted
1 teaspoon vanilla

Preheat oven to 350 degrees. Combine ingredients in order listed. Pour into a 9-by-13-inch pan. Bake for 35-40 minutes.

Icing:

½ cup butter
½ cup sugar

½ cup evaporated milk
1 teaspoon vanilla

Combine ingredients in a small saucepan. Bring to a boil; simmer for 5 minutes. Punch holes in the warm cake with a sharp knife, and spoon the hot mixture over it the cake.

◌ Sock It to Me Cake ◌

1 box butter cake mix
½ cup sugar
4 eggs
1 cup sour cream
¾ cup vegetable oil

1 cup broken pecans
1 teaspoon vanilla
2 tablespoons brown sugar
1 teaspoon sugar

Do not preheat oven. Combine the cake mix, sugar, eggs, sour cream, and oil. Mix well. Pour half the batter into a greased tube pan. Combine the pecans, vanilla, brown sugar, and cinnamon. Sprinkle over the batter in the pan. Pour the rest of the batter over the pecans. Bake at 375 degrees for 1 hour. *This cake does not require any frosting.*

∽ 7-Up Cake ∾

1 box deluxe or lemon supreme
  cake mix
1 (3-ounce) box instant lemon
  pudding mix
½ cup vegetable oil
4 eggs

1 (10-ounce) bottle 7-Up
½ cup margarine
1 small can crushed pineapple,
  undrained
1 cup sugar
1 small can coconut

Preheat oven to 325 degrees. Mix together the cake mix, pudding mix, vegetable oil, eggs, and 7-Up. Grease and flour a 9-by-13-inch pan. Pour batter into the pan. Bake for 40 to 45 minutes. Leave cake in pan for five minutes, then remove from pan and let cool. In a medium saucepan, combine the margarine, pineapple and juice, sugar, and coconut. Bring to a boil; boil for one minute. Remove from heat and pour over cooled cake.

∽ Piña Colada Cake ∾

1 box yellow cake mix
1 can sweetened condensed milk
1 can Piña Colada mix

1 (8-ounce) carton whipped
  topping

Prepare and bake cake according to package instructions in a 9-by-13-inch pan. Punch lots of holes in cake. Pour sweetened condensed milk over cake. Pour Piña Colada mix over cake. Frost with whipped topping. Makes 12 to 15 servings.

∽ Tennessee Black Walnut Cake ∽

½ cup butter, softened
½ cup vegetable shortening
2 cups sugar
5 egg yolks
1 cup buttermilk
1 teaspoon baking soda
2 cups flour
1½ teaspoons vanilla
5 egg whites, stiffly beaten

1 cup chopped black walnuts
1 cup coconut
1 (8-ounce) package cream cheese, softened
¼ cup butter, softened
1 (16-ounce) package powdered sugar
1 teaspoon vanilla

Preheat oven to 350 degrees. Cream butter, shortening, and sugar in bowl until light and fluffy. Beat in egg yolks. Dissolve baking soda in buttermilk. Add flour alternately with buttermilk, mixing well after each addition. Beat in 1½ teaspoons vanilla. Gently fold in egg whites. Fold in walnuts and coconut. Pour into 3 greased-and-floured 8-inch round pans. Bake for 30 minutes. Beat cream cheese and ¼ cup butter in mixing bowl. Add powdered sugar and 1 teaspoon vanilla; beat until of spreading consistency. Spread between layers and over top and sides of cake. Makes 16 servings. *This recipe is at least 200 years old.*

∽ Ooie Gooie Butter Cake ∽

1 box yellow cake mix
1 cup chopped nuts
½ cup butter, melted

3 eggs
1 (16-ounce) box powdered sugar
8 ounces cream cheese

Preheat oven to 350 degrees. Mix together the cake mix, nuts, butter, and one egg. Batter will be thick. Pour into a buttered cake pan. Mix together the powdered sugar, the 2 remaining eggs, and cream cheese; pour over the first mixture. Bake for 30 to 45 minutes.

❧ Coconut Cake ❧

1 box deluxe or supreme white
   cake mix
12 ounces frozen coconut
2 teaspoons coconut flavoring
²/₃ cup evaporated milk

1¹/₃ cups water
¹/₂ cup sugar
1 (14-ounce) container whipped
   topping
1 teaspoon vanilla

Prepare cake in a 9-by-12-inch pan according to package directions, adding ²/₃ cup coconut and 1 teaspoon of the coconut flavoring before baking. Combine the evaporated milk, sugar, 1 teaspoon coconut flavoring, and vanilla. Add enough water to make 2 cups. Punch holes in cake with a round toothpick as soon as it comes out of the oven. Spoon the milk mixture over the cake; cover with whipped topping and the remaining coconut. Makes 12 to 15 servings.

❧ Triple Chocolate Cake ❧

1 (12-ounce) package chocolate
   chips
1 devil's food cake mix
1 cup vegetable oil
1 (3-ounce) package instant milk
   chocolate pudding mix

1 cup sour cream
4 eggs
¹/₂ cup warm water
¹/₄ teaspoon salt
Powdered sugar
Whipped cream

Preheat oven to 350 degrees. Combine the chocolate chips, cake mix, oil, pudding mix, sour cream, eggs, water, and salt in a large bowl. Mix well. Pour into a greased-and-floured Bundt cake pan. Bake for 50 minutes. Remove from oven; let cool. Remove cake from pan and sprinkle with powdered sugar. Serve with whipped cream.

∽ Spicy Gingerbread with Lemon Sauce ∽

3 eggs

1 cup sugar

1 cup oil

1 cup molasses (sorghum is best)

1 teaspoon cloves

1 teaspoon ginger

1 teaspoon cinnamon

½ teaspoon salt

2 teaspoons baking soda

2 tablespoons hot water

2 cups flour

1 cup boiling water

Lemon Sauce

Preheat oven to 375 degrees. Grease and flour a rectangular 9-by-13-inch pan. Combine eggs, sugar, oil, molasses, cloves, ginger, cinnamon, and salt in a large bowl; beat well. Dissolve the baking soda in 2 tablespoons hot water; add to the beaten mixture. Sift in flour and beat well. Add 1 cup boiling water. Beat lightly and quickly. Pour batter into prepared pan. *Do not add more flour.* Bake for 45 minutes. Serve with Lemon Sauce. Makes 10 to 12 servings.

Lemon Sauce:

1 cup sugar

4 tablespoons flour or

   2 tablespoons cornstarch

2 cups boiling water

3 tablespoons butter

3 tablespoons lemon juice

2 teaspoons grated lemon rind

Combine sugar and flour. Whisk sugar mixture into boiling water. Cook until thick and rather clear, stirring as needed to make smooth, about 10 minutes. Remove from heat and add the butter, lemon juice, and rind. Blend well. Makes about 2½ cups.

‰ "Lindsey" Chocolate Chip Bundt Cake ‰

1 butter-flavored yellow cake mix
1 (3-ounce) package instant
   chocolate pudding mix
¾ cup vegetable oil
4 eggs

1 tablespoon vanilla
¼ cup water
1 (8-ounce) carton sour cream
1 (6-ounce) package mini
   chocolate chips

Preheat oven to 350 degrees. Mix yellow cake mix and chocolate pudding together in a large mixing bowl. Make a well; add oil, eggs, vanilla, water, and sour cream. Beat with electric mixer for about 2 minutes. Fold in mini chocolate chips. Pour into a greased Bundt pan. Bake for 1 hour. *This is a never-fail recipe.*

‰ Earthquake Cake ‰

1 cup coconut
1 cup pecans
1 German chocolate cake mix

1 cup butter
8 ounces cream cheese
1 (16-ounce) box powdered sugar

Preheat oven to 350 degrees. Spray a 9-by-13-inch pan with cooking spray. Layer coconut and pecans in pan. Prepare cake mix according to package directions; pour over coconut and pecans. Cream butter and cream cheese; mix in powdered sugar. Swirl cream cheese mixture over cake batter. Bake for 35 minutes. Do not overbake. *This cake looks like an earthquake and is good served with ice cream or whipped topping.*

∽ Jam Cake ∽

1 box cake mix	1 cup chopped pecans
1 cup raisins	1 cup blackberry jam

Prepare cake mix according to package directions. Add the raisins, pecans, and jam to batter. Mix well with an electric mixer. Grease a cake pan well with butter. Cut out waxed paper to put in bottom of cake pan; grease this also. Bake according to cake mix directions.

∽ Five-Flavor Cake ∽

1 cup butter or margarine	1 teaspoon coconut extract
1/2 cup vegetable shortening	1 teaspoon rum extract
3 cups sugar	1 teaspoon lemon extract
5 eggs, well beaten	1 teaspoon butter extract
3 cups flour	1 teaspoon vanilla
1/2 teaspoon baking powder	Five-Flavor Glaze
1 cup milk	

Preheat oven to 325 degrees. Cream the butter, shortening, and sugar until light and fluffy. Add eggs. Combine the flour and baking powder; add to creamed mixture alternately with the milk. Stir in flavorings. Spoon mixture into a greased 10-inch tube pan and bake for about 1 1/2 hours or until cake tests done. Add Five-Flavor Glaze and cool in pan for about 10 minutes before turning out on a rack to cool.

Five-Flavor Glaze:

1/2 cup sugar	1/4 teaspoon each coconut, rum,
1/4 cup water	butter, lemon, vanilla extract

Combine ingredients in a heavy saucepan. Bring to a boil and stir until sugar is dissolved. Pour over hot cake in pan. Allow glazed cake to cool in pan before turning out.

◠ Raspberry-Walnut Torte ◠

1¼ cups flour
⅓ cup powdered sugar
½ cup butter, softened
10 ounces frozen raspberries, thawed and drained, juice reserved
¾ cup chopped walnuts

2 eggs
1 cup sugar
½ teaspoon salt
½ teaspoon baking powder
1 teaspoon vanilla
Raspberry Sauce

Preheat oven to 350 degrees. Combine 1 cup of the flour, powdered sugar, and butter. Press mixture into a 9-by-13-inch pan. Bake for 15 minutes. Cool. Spoon raspberries over crust. Sprinkle with walnuts. Beat eggs and sugar until fluffy. Add salt, the remaining 1/4 cup flour, baking powder, and vanilla. Blend well. Pour over walnuts. Bake for 30 to 35 minutes, or until brown. Cool. Cut into squares. Serve with whipped topping and Raspberry Sauce.

Raspberry Sauce:

Reserved raspberry juice
½ cup sugar
½ cup water

2 tablespoons cornstarch
1 tablespoon lemon juice

Mix the raspberry juice, sugar, water, and cornstarch together in a saucepan. Cook, stirring constantly, until thick and clear. Stir in lemon juice. Cool.

⌒ Buttermilk Cake ⌒

1 cup butter
3 cups sugar
5 eggs, well beaten
1 cup buttermilk
1/4 teaspoon baking soda

3 cups flour
1 teaspoon vanilla
1 teaspoon orange flavoring
1 teaspoon almond extract

Preheat oven to 325 degrees. Cream the butter and sugar well, adding the sugar gradually so that mixture is not grainy. Add the eggs. Mix thoroughly. Stir the baking soda into buttermilk. Add the buttermilk mixture and flour alternately to the sugar mixture. Add the vanilla, orange flavoring, and almond extract. Pour into a well-greased-and-floured tube pan. Bake for about 1 1/2 hours. Turn out on rack to cool. Serve plain with fruit, or glaze with your favorite glaze. *This cake may be frozen.*

⌒ Amaretto Cake ⌒

1 cup butter
1/2 cup vegetable shortening
3 cups sugar
5 eggs
3 cups flour
1/2 teaspoon baking powder

1/2 teaspoon salt
1 cup milk
1 tablespoon vanilla
1 tablespoon Amaretto liqueur
1 to 2 teaspoons almond extract

Preheat oven to 325 degrees. Cream the butter, shortening, and sugar. Add the eggs one at a time, beating after each addition. Combine the flour, baking powder, and salt. Add flour mixture and milk alternately to butter mixture. Add the vanilla, Amaretto liqueur, and almond extract. Bake in a greased-and-floured tube pan for 70 minutes.

☙ Vasilopita ❧

3/4 cup butter
3/4 cup sugar
4 eggs
1/2 cup orange juice
1/2 teaspoon baking soda
3 teaspoons lemon juice

1 teaspoon vanilla
3 teaspoons baking powder
3 cups flour
1/3 cup milk
1/2 cup chopped walnuts

Preheat oven to 350 degrees. Cream butter and sugar. Add the eggs one at a time, beating well. Stir the baking soda into the orange juice; add to the sugar mixture. Add the lemon juice and vanilla. Combine the baking powder and sifted flour. Add a little of the flour mixture to the sugar mixture. Add a little of the milk to the sugar mixture. Continue adding flour and milk and blend well. Stir in walnuts. Bake for 50 to 60 minutes. *Vasilopita is the traditional Greek New Year's Day cake. The custom is to insert a coin into the underside of the cold cake by making a small cut with a pointed knife. The cake is sliced, and tradition has it that the person receiving the slice with the coin will be blessed with good luck for the entire year.*

☙ Apple Cake ❧

3 cups sliced apples
1 1/2 cups sugar
1/2 cup vegetable oil
1/2 cup nuts
1 teaspoon cinnamon
1/2 teaspoon nutmeg

1 teaspoon vanilla
2 eggs, beaten
3/4 teaspoon salt
2 cups flour
1 1/2 teaspoons baking soda

Preheat the oven to 325 degrees. Combine the apples, sugar, oil, nuts, cinnamon, nutmeg, and vanilla. Pour eggs over the apple mixture. Mix well. Add the salt, flour, and baking soda to the apple mixture. Mix well. Grease and flour a 9-by-13-inch pan. Pour batter into pan; bake for 50 to 60 minutes. *If desired, use two 8-by-8-inch pans and bake for 40 minutes.*

WCN Fresh Apple Nut Cake

2 eggs	1 cup chopped walnuts
1¾ cups sugar	3 cups chopped peeled apples
1 cup vegetable oil	1 teaspoon cinnamon
2½ cups sifted self-rising flour	1 teaspoon vanilla

Preheat oven to 300 degrees. Grease a 9-by-13-inch baking pan. Combine the eggs, sugar, and oil in a bowl; blend well. Gradually add flour; blend well. Stir in walnuts, apples, cinnamon, and vanilla; blend well. Pour into prepared pan. Bake for 1 hour and 10 minutes or until a toothpick inserted in the center comes out clean.

WCN Fresh Apple Cake

4 cups fresh apples, chopped fine	½ teaspoon salt
2 cups sugar	2 teaspoons baking soda
1 cup chopped pecans	1 cup vegetable oil
2 cups flour	1 teaspoon vanilla
½ teaspoon cinnamon	2 eggs, well beaten

Mix apples, sugar, and pecans in a large bowl. Let stand for 1 hour, stirring often. Preheat oven to 350 degrees. Add the flour, cinnamon, salt, and baking soda to the apple mixture. Add the oil, vanilla, and eggs. Stir by hand until well mixed. Pour into a greased-and-floured tube pan. Bake for 1 hour and 15 minutes.

❧ Apple Cake II ❧

1½ cups vegetable oil	1 teaspoon baking soda
2 cups sugar	3 cups sliced apples
3 large eggs	1½ cups nuts
2 teaspoons vanilla	1 cup brown sugar
3 cups sifted flour	½ cup margarine
1 teaspoon salt	¼ cup evaporated milk

Preheat oven to 325 degrees. Combine the oil, sugar, eggs, 1 teaspoon vanilla, flour, salt, baking soda, apples, and nuts in the order listed. Mix in order. Bake in a rectangular pan for 1 hour. When cake has almost finished baking, prepare the glaze: In a saucepan, combine the brown sugar, margarine, evaporated milk, and remaining 1 teaspoon vanilla. Bring mixture to a boil; boil for 2½ minutes. Pour over hot cake.

❧ Sour Cream Coconut Cake ❧

1 (18½-ounce) box Duncan Hines Golden Recipe cake mix	1 (12-ounce) package frozen coconut
2 cups sugar	8 ounces whipped topping
16 ounces sour cream	

Bake the cake according package instructions for 2 round layers. Let cool. Split the 2 layers to make 4 layers. Combine the sugar, sour cream, and coconut. Mix well. Reserve 1 cup of this mixture for icing. Spread the remaining mixture between and on top of 3 layers of the cake. Place the top layer on the cake. Combine the whipped topping and reserved 1 cup of coconut mixture; ice the cake. Seal the cake well with icing; it should be thick on top. Store in an airtight container in the refrigerator. *This cake keeps well. It tastes best if made one day in advance.*

⌒ Snowball Cake ⌒

2 envelopes unflavored gelatin
4 tablespoons cold water
1 cup boiling water
1 cup pineapple juice
1 cup sugar
Juice of 1 lemon

1 small angel food cake, broken
  into small pieces
1 cup crushed, drained pineapple
2 (8-ounce) cartons whipped
  topping
Coconut to taste

In a large bowl, stir together the gelatin and cold water. Add the boiling water, pineapple juice, sugar, and lemon juice. Chill until mixture begins to gel; remove from refrigerator and beat until foamy. Fold in the angel food cake pieces, crushed pineapple, and 1 carton whipped topping. Pour into a 9-by-13-inch glass dish. Spread with the remaining carton of whipped topping; sprinkle with coconut.

∽ Wine-Pecan Cake ∽

3 cups flour
1 pound crystallized cherries
1 pound crystallized pineapple
1 cup butter
2 cups sugar
6 eggs, beaten

1/2 teaspoon salt
2 teaspoons baking powder
1 teaspoon nutmeg
1/2 cup wine
1 pound pecans

Preheat oven to 300 degrees. Dredge the cherries and pineapples in 1 cup of the flour. Set aside. Cream the butter and sugar. Add the eggs. Add the remaining 2 cups flour, salt, baking powder, and nutmeg. Stir in the cherries, pineapple, and pecans. Pour into baking pan; bake for 1 hour and 45 minutes. *If necessary, put a pan of water on the lower rack of the oven beneath the cake to keep the bottom from becoming too brown.*

∽ Old-Fashioned Fruit Cake ∽

4 eggs
1 cup sugar
1 cup flour
1/2 teaspoon salt
1/2 teaspoon baking powder

1/2 pound crystallized pineapple
1 pound chopped dates
1 pound pecans
1 pound crystallized cherries, chopped

Preheat oven to 300 degrees. Cream the eggs and sugar well. Combine the flour, salt, and baking powder. Add the pineapple, dates, pecans, and cherries to the flour mixture. Add the egg mixture to the flour mixture. Grease 2 (9-inch) loaf pans; line with waxed paper. Spoon batter into prepared pans. Bake for 1 hour and 10 minutes. Let cool; remove from pans.

∞ Spicy Fruit Cake ∞

1 cup butter
1 cup sugar
4 eggs
Grated rind and juice of
   1/2 lemon
Grated rind and juice of
   1/2 orange
1/2 cup apple jelly or raspberry
   jam
1 box seedless raisins

1 box currants
1/2 pound citron
1/2 pound cherries
1/2 pound pecans, chopped
2 cups flour
3 teaspoons baking powder
1/2 teaspoon salt
1/2 teaspoon cinnamon
1/2 teaspoon ground cloves
1/2 teaspoon mace

Preheat oven to 325 degrees. Grease a Bundt pan well and line
with heavy waxed paper that has also been greased. Cream the
butter, sugar, and eggs together until creamy and fluffy. Sift
1 1/2 cups of the flour together with the baking powder, salt,
cinnamon, ground cloves, and mace. In a separate bowl,
combine the jelly and fruit juices. Add the jelly and flour
mixtures alternately to the butter mixture. Dredge the raisins,
currants, citron, and cherries in the remaining 1/2 cup of
flour. Add the floured fruits and the pecans to the batter;
mix well. Turn batter into prepared pan. Bake for 2 1/2 hours.
Makes 1 (8-pound) cake. *This cake may be baked in a loaf pan.*

WCN Mother's White Fruit Cake

4 cups shelled pecans
3/4 pound candied cherries
1 pound candied pineapple
1 3/4 cups all-purpose flour
1 cup butter

1 cup sugar
5 large eggs, well beaten
1/2 teaspoon baking powder
1 tablespoon vanilla
1 tablespoon lemon extract

Do not preheat oven. Chop the pecans, cherries, and pineapple into medium-sized pieces; dredge with 1/4 cup of the flour. Cream butter and sugar together until light and fluffy. Add eggs; blend well. Sift remaining flour and baking powder together; fold into butter mixture. Add vanilla and lemon extract; mix well. Add pecans, cherries, and pineapple, blending in well. Grease a 10-inch tube pan; line with paper and grease again. Pour batter into prepared pan. Place in a cold oven and bake at 250 degrees for 3 hours. Cool in pan on cake rack. Makes one 5-pound cake.

Chocolate Cherry Cake

1 box chocolate cake mix
2 eggs, beaten
1 can cherry pie filling
1/4 teaspoon almond extract

1 cup sugar
5 tablespoons butter
1/3 cup evaporated milk
1 cup chocolate chips

Preheat oven to 325 degrees. Combine the cake mix, eggs, cherry pie filling, and almond extract. Mix well by hand until good and moist. Pour into 2 layer pans or 1 sheet pan. Bake for about 50 minutes or until tester comes out dry. While cake is baking, combine the sugar, butter, and evaporated milk in a saucepan. Bring to a boil; boil for one minute. Remove from heat; stir in the chocolate chips. Beat until smooth. Remove cake from oven; let cool. Ice cake with chocolate icing.

∞ Pumpkin Cake ∞

1 package yellow cake mix
2 eggs
¼ cup water
2 teaspoons baking soda
1 teaspoon cinnamon

½ teaspoon ginger
¼ teaspoon ground cloves
1 (16-ounce) can pumpkin
Whipped cream to taste

Preheat oven to 350 degrees. In a large mixing bowl, combine the cake mix, eggs, water, baking soda, cinnamon, ginger, ground cloves, and pumpkin in the order listed. Beat with an electric mixer for four minutes at medium speed. Pour the batter into a greased-and-floured Bundt or tube cake pan. Bake for 30 to 35 minutes or until cake tests done. Cool for 10 minutes before removing from pan. Serve with whipped cream. Makes 10 to 12 servings. *This is a good cake for autumn.*

∞ Pineapple Nut Cake ∞

1 (3-ounce) can crushed pineapple
1 cup brown sugar
1 box yellow cake mix, dry

¾ cup unsalted butter
1 to 2 cups chopped pecans

Preheat oven to 350 degrees. Grease an 11-by-13-inch glass baking dish. Spread the pineapple over the bottom of the dish. Spread the brown sugar over the pineapple. Sprinkle the cake mix over the brown sugar. Slice the butter and place over cake mix. Top with pecans. Bake for 30 to 45 minutes, until pecans look almost burned.

❧ Buttermilk Pound Cake ❧

1 cup butter, or ½ cup margarine
and ½ cup vegetable shortening
3 cups sugar
5 eggs
½ teaspoon baking soda

1 tablespoon boiling water
1 cup buttermilk
3 cups flour
Pinch of salt
2 teaspoons vanilla

Preheat oven to 350 degrees. Cream butter and sugar. Add eggs and beat well. Dissolve baking soda in boiling water and add to buttermilk. Add buttermilk and flour alternately to the sugar mixture. Add salt and vanilla. Pour into 2 well-greased-and-floured loaf pans (or one tube pan, if desired). Bake for about 1 hour and 10 minutes. Cool in pan.

❧ Lemon Pound Cake ❧

1½ cups butter
3 cups sugar
3 cups flour

¾ cup 7-Up
3 tablespoons lemon extract
5 eggs

Preheat oven to 350 degrees. Combine ingredients. Mix well. Pour batter into a Bundt pan; bake for 70 minutes.

∽ Pound Cake ∽

2 sticks butter, softened
3 cups sugar
6 eggs, separated
2 teaspoons vanilla
3 teaspoons almond extract

1 teaspoon lemon extract
3½ cups cake flour
¼ teaspoon baking soda
½ pint sour cream

Preheat oven to 300 or 325 degrees. Cream the butter and sugar; add the egg yolks one at a time. Add the vanilla, almond extract, and lemon extract. Combine the flour and baking soda. Add the flour mixture and sour cream alternately to the butter mixture. Beat the egg whites until stiff; fold gently into the batter. Pour into a greased pan. Bake for 1½ hours.

WCN Cream Cheese Pound Cake

3 cups sugar
1½ cups margarine
1 (8-ounce) package cream cheese
6 large eggs

1 teaspoon vanilla
½ teaspoon salt
3 cups flour

Do not preheat oven. Cream the sugar, margarine, and cream cheese. Add the eggs one at a time, beating after each addition. Add the vanilla and salt, mixing at a slower speed. Add the flour a little at a time. Pour batter into a large, floured stem pan. Put in cold oven. Turn oven on to 300 degrees. Bake for 1½ hours.

ᔓ Chocolate Pound Cake ᔔ

1 cup margarine
½ cup vegetable shortening
3 cups sugar
3 cups flour
½ cup cocoa
½ teaspoon baking powder

1 teaspoon salt
5 eggs
1 cup milk
1½ teaspoons vanilla
Chocolate Icing

Preheat oven to 325 degrees. Cream the margarine and shortening. Gradually add the sugar; cream well. Sift together the flour, cocoa, baking powder, and salt; set aside. Add the eggs one at a time to the creamed mixture, beating after each addition. Alternately add the flour mixture and the milk. Stir in the vanilla. Pour into a greased and lightly floured 10-by-4-inch tube pan. Bake for 1 hour and 15 minutes. Let cool before removing from pan. Ice cake with Chocolate Icing. *This cake stays moist for days.*

Chocolate Icing:

6 tablespoons margarine
5 tablespoons cocoa
1 box powdered sugar

5 tablespoons milk
1 teaspoon vanilla

Cream the margarine. Combine the cocoa and powdered sugar; add alternately with the milk to the margarine. Add the vanilla. Mix well.

⚭ Coconut Pound Cake ⚭

½ cup butter	3 cups flour
½ cup margarine	1 cup milk
½ cup vegetable shortening	1 tablespoon coconut extract
3 cups sugar	1 teaspoon almond extract
6 eggs	1 can flaked coconut

Do not preheat oven. Cream the butter, margarine, shortening, and sugar well. Add the eggs one at a time, beating for 2 minutes after each addition. Add the flour and milk alternately to the creamed mixture. Blend in the coconut extract, almond extract, and flaked coconut. Pour batter into a large stem pan or 3 loaf pans. Bake at 350 degrees for 1 to 1¹/₄ hours. Test for doneness before removing from pan.

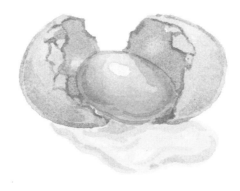

∞ Best Cheesecake ∞

1½ cups graham cracker crumbs
½ cup butter, melted
⅓ cup powdered sugar
¼ teaspoon cinnamon
3 (8-ounce) packages cream cheese, softened (may use low-fat)
4 eggs

1 cup sugar
1 teaspoon vanilla
¼ teaspoon almond extract (optional)
2 cups sour cream, at room temperature
1 (21-ounce) can cherry or blueberry pie filling

Preheat oven to 350 degrees. Combine the graham cracker crumbs, butter, powdered sugar, and cinnamon. Press into the bottom of a springform pan. In a large mixing bowl beat the cream cheese, eggs, sugar, vanilla, and almond extract until smooth. Pour over prepared crust. Bake for 30 minutes. Remove from oven. Spread the sour cream on top of the cake; bake for 5 more minutes. Remove from oven and let cool. Spread pie filling on top. Chill overnight. Carefully remove sides from pan and serve. Makes 16 servings.

WCN Coconut Macaroon Cheesecake

1⅓ cup flaked toasted coconut

½ cup ground pecans

2 tablespoons butter or margarine, melted

3 (8-ounce) packages cream cheese, softened

½ cup sugar

1 teaspoon vanilla

⅓ teaspoon almond extract

3 eggs

1 egg white

⅓ cup sugar

Preheat oven to 350 degrees. In a small bowl combine 1 cup of the toasted coconut, ground pecans, and melted butter. Press into the bottom of a 9-inch springform pan. Set aside. In large mixing bowl, beat the cream cheese with an electric mixer on low speed; gradually add the ½ cup sugar, ½ teaspoon vanilla, and almond extract. Beat until fluffy. Add 3 eggs; beat on low speed just until combined. Pour into crust-lined pan. Bake for 35 minutes. (Cheesecake will not be completely done at this point.) In a small mixing bowl, beat the egg white and remaining ½ teaspoon vanilla with an electric mixer until soft peaks form. Gradually beat in the ⅓ cup sugar until stiff peaks form. Fold in the remaining ⅓ cup toasted coconut. Carefully spread over top of partially baked cheesecake. Return to oven and bake for 20 minutes longer. Cool on wire rack for 15 minutes. Loosen sides of cheesecake from pan. Cool for 30 minutes more; remove sides of pan. Cool completely. Cover and chill for at least 4 hours before serving. Makes 12 to 16 servings. *Before serving, garnish with strawberries and additional toasted coconut, if desired.*

∽ Delectable Cheesecake ∾

1¼ cups crushed graham crackers
⅓ cup butter, melted
1¼ cups sugar
4 large packages cream cheese,
    room temperature

3 large eggs, room temperature
1 tablespoon vanilla

Preheat oven to 350 degrees. Mix together the crushed graham crackers, butter, and ¼ cup sugar. Press mixture onto the bottom and sides of a springform pan. Combine the cream cheese, eggs, vanilla, and remaining 1 cup sugar; blend until mixture is smooth and all lumps are gone. Pour into prepared crust and bake for about 70 minutes. *To help keep cheesecake moist, place a pan of water in the oven during baking. To make a chocolate cheesecake, combine 2 squares of semisweet chocolate and 1 tablespoon of water in a double boiler; stir until chocolate is melted. Add to the cheesecake batter.*

WCN Mississippi Mud Cake

1 cup margarine
2 cups sugar
½ cup cocoa
4 large eggs

1½ cups self-rising flour
1 cup pecans
1 cup coconut
7 ounces marshmallow creme

Preheat oven to 250 to 300 degrees. Combine the margarine, sugar, cocoa, eggs, flour, pecans, and coconut. Mix well. Bake for 50 minutes. Spread the marshmallow creme on top of cooled cake.

WCN Italian Cream Cake

½ cup margarine	1 teaspoon vanilla
½ cup vegetable shortening	1 small can flaked coconut
2 cups sugar	1 cup chopped pecans
5 egg yolks	5 egg whites, beaten
2 cups flour	Cream Cheese Frosting
1 teaspoon baking soda	Chopped pecans for topping
1 cup buttermilk	

Preheat oven to 350 degrees. Using an electric mixer, beat the margarine and shortening together. Add the sugar and beat well. Add the egg yolks one at a time. Sift the flour and baking soda together; add alternately with the buttermilk to the shortening mixture. Add the vanilla, coconut, and pecans. Fold in beaten egg whites. Pour into 3 (8- or 9-inch) greased-and-floured pans. Bake for 45 minutes or until sides break loose. Leave in pans until cool. Frost cake with Cream Cheese Frosting. Sprinkle sides and top with chopped pecans.

Cream Cheese Frosting:

¼ cup margarine	1 box powdered sugar
1 (8-ounce) package cream cheese	1 teaspoon vanilla

Cream margarine and cream cheese together; add sugar and vanilla and beat well.

WCN Hummingbird Cake

3 cups flour
2 cups sugar
1 teaspoon salt
1 teaspoon baking soda
1 teaspoon cinnamon
3 eggs, beaten
1 cup vegetable oil

2 teaspoons vanilla
1 (8-ounce) can crushed
   pineapple, undrained
1 cup chopped pecans
2 cups chopped bananas
Cream Cheese Frosting

Preheat oven to 350 degrees. Combine the flour, sugar, salt, baking soda, and cinnamon in a large mixing bowl. Add eggs and oil, stirring until dry ingredients are moistened. Do not beat. Stir in the vanilla, pineapple, pecans, and bananas. Spoon batter into 3 well-greased-and-floured cake pans. Bake for 25 to 30 minutes or until cake tests done. Cool in pans for 10 minutes; remove from pans and cool completely. Spread frosting between layers and on top and sides of cake.

Cream Cheese Frosting:

2 (8-ounce) packages cream
   cheese, softened
1 cup butter, softened

2 (16-ounce) packages powdered
   sugar
2 teaspoons vanilla

Combine cream cheese and butter; cream until smooth. Add powdered sugar, beating until light and fluffy. Stir in vanilla.

WCN German Sweet Chocolate Cake

1 (4-ounce) package sweet baking chocolate
1/2 cup water
2 cups flour
1 teaspoon baking soda
1/4 teaspoon salt
1 cup butter or margarine, softened
2 cups sugar
4 egg yolks
1 teaspoon vanilla
1 cup buttermilk
4 egg whites
Coconut-Pecan Frosting (recipe follows)

Preheat oven to 350 degrees. Line bottoms of 3 (9-inch) round cake pans with waxed paper. Microwave chocolate and water in large microwavable bowl on high for 1¹/₂ to 2 minutes, or until chocolate is almost melted. *(For top-of-stove preparation, heat chocolate and water in heavy 1-quart saucepan on very low heat, stirring constantly, until chocolate is melted and mixture is smooth. Remove from heat.)* Combine flour, baking soda, and salt; set aside. Beat butter and sugar in large bowl with electric mixer on medium speed until light and fluffy. Add egg yolks, one at a time, beating well after each addition. Stir in chocolate mixture and vanilla. Add flour mixture alternately with buttermilk, beating after each addition until smooth. Beat egg whites in another large bowl with electric mixer on high speed until stiff peaks form. Gently stir egg whites into batter. Pour into prepared pans. Bake for 30 minutes, or until cake springs back when lightly touched in center. Immediately run spatula between cakes and sides of pans. Cool for 15 minutes; remove from pans. Remove waxed paper. Cool completely on wire racks. Spread Coconut-Pecan Frosting between layers and over top of cakes. Makes 12 servings.

Coconut-Pecan Frosting:

1 (12-ounce) can evaporated milk	1½ teaspoons vanilla
½ cup sugar	1 (7-ounce) package flaked
¾ cup butter or margarine	coconut
4 egg whites, slightly beaten	1½ cups chopped pecans

Mix milk, sugar, butter, egg whites, and vanilla in large saucepan. Cook and stir over medium heat for about 12 minutes, or until thickened and golden brown. Remove from heat. Stir in coconut and pecans. Beat until cool and of spreading consistency. Makes 4¼ cups.

WCN Orange Chiffon Cake

2¼ cups sifted cake flour	2 teaspoons grated orange rind
1 tablespoon baking powder	¾ cup orange juice
½ teaspoon salt	1 teaspoon vanilla
1½ cups sugar	8 egg whites
½ cup vegetable oil	½ teaspoon cream of tartar
5 egg yolks	

Preheat oven to 325 degrees. Combine the flour, baking powder, salt, and sugar in a mixing bowl. Make a well in center; add the oil, egg yolks, orange rind, orange juice, and vanilla. Beat at medium speed with an electric mixer until smooth. Beat egg whites and cream of tartar in a large mixing bowl at high speed until soft peaks form. Pour egg yolk mixture in a thin, steady stream over egg whites; gently fold yolks into whites. Pour batter into an ungreased 10-inch tube pan, spreading evenly. Bake for 1 hour or until cake springs back when lightly touched. Invert pan; cool for 40 minutes. Loosen cake from sides of pan, using a narrow metal spatula; remove from pan.

WCN Lemon Daffodil Torte

1 (14-ounce) can sweetened condensed milk (not evaporated milk)
1/2 cup lemon juice
1/2 teaspoon grated lemon rind
Yellow food coloring
2 cups flour
1 tablespoon baking powder
1/2 teaspoon salt

1 1/2 cups sugar
3/4 cup vegetable shortening
2 teaspoons vanilla
1 cup milk
4 egg whites
Creamy White Frosting

3/4 cup flaked coconut

Preheat oven to 350 degrees. In medium bowl, combine sweetened condensed milk, lemon juice, lemon rind, and food coloring. Chill. Meanwhile, combine flour, baking powder, and salt. In large bowl, beat sugar, shortening, and vanilla until fluffy. Add flour mixture alternately with milk to the shortening mixture, beating well. In small bowl, beat egg whites until stiff but not dry. Fold into batter. Spread into 2 greased-and-floured 8- or 9-inch round layer cake pans. Bake for 25 minutes or until wooden pick comes out clean. Cool for 10 minutes. Remove from pans; cool completely. Split each layer horizontally into 2 layers. Spread about 1/2 cup lemon mixture between each layer and over top to within 1 inch of edge. Frost side and 1-inch rim with Creamy White Frosting. Coat side of cake with coconut. Store covered in refrigerator.

Creamy White Frosting:

1 cup powdered sugar
2/3 cup vegetable shortening

2 tablespoons milk
1 teaspoon vanilla

Combine ingredients; beat on low speed until smooth. Add additional milk, if needed, for desired consistency.

WCN Strawberry Cake

1 package white cake mix	½ cup water
1 package strawberry-flavored	4 eggs
gelatin	1 cup frozen strawberries
1 cup vegetable oil	½ cup nuts

Preheat oven to 350 degrees. Blend together cake mix, gelatin, oil, water, and eggs; beat at medium speed for 2 minutes. Add strawberries and nuts. Bake for one hour.

WCN Texas Tornado Cake

1½ cups sugar	2 cups all-purpose flour
2 eggs	¾ cup self-rising flour
2 cups fruit cocktail, liquid	¼ cup brown sugar
included	1 cup chopped nuts
2 teaspoons baking soda	

Preheat oven to 325 degrees. Cream together the sugar, eggs, fruit cocktail, baking soda, all-purpose flour, and self-rising flour. Pour into a lightly greased-and-floured 9-by-13-inch pan. Mix the brown sugar and nuts together; sprinkle over the batter. Bake for 40 minutes. Spread with favorite icing.

WCN Glory Be Cake

1 cup self-rising flour	3 eggs
2 cups sugar	1 (7¾-ounce) jar junior baby
2 tablespoons powdered instant	food prunes
tea	1 cup chopped pecans
1 cup vegetable oil	

Preheat oven to 350 degrees. Combine all ingredients in large mixing bowl. Beat for only about 30 seconds. Pour into a tube pan. Bake for 65 minutes.

175

WCN Prune Cake

1 1/2 cups sugar
1 cup vegetable oil
3 eggs, beaten
2 cups sifted flour
1 teaspoon salt
1 teaspoon baking soda

1 cup buttermilk
1 cup chopped nuts
1 cup cooked chopped prunes
1 teaspoon vanilla
Buttermilk Icing

Preheat oven to 350 degrees. Combine the sugar and oil. Add the eggs. Mix together the flour, salt, and baking soda; add alternately with the buttermilk to the egg mixture, blending well. Fold in the chopped nuts, prunes, and vanilla. Turn into a greased tube pan. Bake for about 50 minutes or until cake tests done. Slowly pour Buttermilk Icing over cake. Icing will turn brown and harden.

Buttermilk Icing:

1 cup sugar
1/2 cup buttermilk
1/2 cup margarine

1/2 teaspoon baking soda
1 teaspoon white corn syrup

Combine ingredients in a saucepan. Cook over medium heat until soft ball stage. Let cool.

⧼ Easy Caramel Icing ⧽

1 pound Kraft caramel
   kisses
1/2 cup milk

1 pound powdered sugar, sifted
1/3 stick (almost 3 tablespoons)
   margarine

Combine the caramel kisses and milk in a double boiler; cook until melted. Add the powdered sugar and margarine. If icing is too thick, add a little more milk (1 tablespoon at a time).

⊙ Never-Fail Frosting ⊙

½ cup water

¼ cup light corn syrup

3 cups sugar

½ teaspoon cream of tartar

4 egg whites

1 teaspoon vanilla

1 scant cup powdered sugar

In a saucepan, heat the water, corn syrup, and sugar until mixture spins a thread. Remove from heat; add the cream of tartar. Beat the egg whites until stiff but not dry. Pour syrup mixture over the egg whites. Add the vanilla. Gradually add the powdered sugar. Makes enough icing for 2 cakes. *Leftover icing can be stored in the refrigerator for later use.*

⊙ Chocolate Icing ⊙

1½ cups sugar

2 tablespoons cocoa

4 tablespoons butter

1 tablespoon light corn syrup

⅓ cup milk

1 teaspoon vanilla

Combine the sugar, cocoa, butter, corn syrup, and milk in a saucepan. Bring to a rolling boil; boil for 1 minute. Add the vanilla. Let cool; beat well.

☙ Almond Pecan Pie ❧

1 cup light corn syrup	¾ stick butter
½ cup sugar	½ cup chopped pecans
2 tablespoons flour	1 teaspoon vanilla
2 eggs, well beaten	½ teaspoon almond extract
¼ teaspoon salt	1 unbaked pie shell

Preheat oven to 350 degrees. Combine the corn syrup, sugar, flour, eggs, salt, butter, pecans, vanilla, and almond extract. Pour into pie shell. Bake for 50 minutes.

☙ French Coconut Pie ❧

½ cup butter, melted	1 teaspoon vanilla
3 eggs, beaten slightly	1 cup flaked coconut
1½ cups sugar	1 unbaked pie shell
1 tablespoon vinegar	

Preheat oven to 350 degrees. Combine the butter, eggs, sugar, vinegar, vanilla, and coconut. Mix well. Pour into pie shell and bake for 1 hour. Cool thoroughly.

☙ Ann's Fudge Pie ❧

1 cup sugar	½ cup margarine or butter,
¼ cup sifted flour	melted
¼ cup cocoa	½ teaspoon vanilla
2 eggs, beaten	

Preheat oven to 350 degrees. Combine ingredients. Bake for 25 minutes.

ᣟ Millionaire Pie ᣞ

1 (13-ounce) carton whipped
  topping
1 can condensed milk
¼ cup lemon juice
1 (20-ounce) can crushed
  pineapple

1 cup chopped pecans or
  walnuts
4 ounces coconut
2 graham cracker pie crusts

Combine the whipped topping, condensed milk, lemon juice, pineapple, nuts, and coconut. Mix well. Pour into pie crusts. Chill in refrigerator for several hours before serving. Makes 12 servings.

ᣟ Pecan Pie ᣞ

2 tablespoons flour
½ cup sugar
3 eggs, beaten slightly
¼ cup butter, softened

½ cup pecans
1 cup light corn syrup
1 tablespoon vanilla
1 unbaked pie shell

Preheat oven to 375 degrees. Combine flour and sugar. Add eggs. Add butter and pecans. Mix well. Pour into unbaked pie shell. Bake for 10 minutes. Reduce oven temperature to 250 degrees and bake for 50 minutes more.

◌⊙ Chocolate Chip Pecan Pie ⊙◌

3 eggs, slightly beaten
1¼ cups corn syrup
⅛ teaspoon salt
1 teaspoon vanilla
½ cup sugar

½ cup pecans, chopped
1 (6-ounce) package chocolate chips
1 (9-inch) unbaked pie shell
Whipped cream (optional)

Preheat oven to 375 degrees. Combine the eggs, corn syrup, salt, vanilla, and sugar. Mix well. Stir in the pecans and chocolate chips. Pour mixture into pie shell. Bake for 55 minutes or until pie is set. Serve with whipped cream if desired.

◌⊙ Blueberry Pie ⊙◌

1 box powdered sugar
1 (8-ounce) package cream cheese
2 envelopes whipped topping mix

1 cup cold milk
2 baked, cooled pie shells
1 can blueberry pie filling

Beat the powdered sugar and cream cheese together in a small mixing bowl. In a large bowl, combine the whipped topping mix and cold milk. Mix on high speed for 2 minutes, until peaks form. Add the cream cheese mixture to the milk mixture. Mix well. Pour into the pie shells. Top with blueberry pie filling. Chill.

☙ Lemonade Pie ❧

1 small can frozen lemonade
  concentrate
1 can sweetened condensed milk
1 (20-ounce) can crushed
  pineapple, drained

1 cup chopped pecans
1 (12-ounce) carton whipped
  topping
2 graham cracker pie crusts

Blend lemonade and sweetened condensed milk until well
thickened. Add pineapple and pecans. Blend well. Fold in
whipped topping. Pour into 2 graham cracker pie crusts. Chill
well. *This is a good summer dessert.*

☙ Apple Pie ❧

3 cups apples, sliced
1 cup sugar
¾ stick butter
¾ cup orange juice

¾ teaspoon cinnamon
2½ to 3 tablespoons flour
Dough for 2 pie crusts

Preheat oven to 425 degrees. Combine ingredients in a large
saucepan. Bring to a boil; boil for 2 minutes. Line a 10-inch pan
with half the dough. Pour apples into the pan. Cut remaining
dough into strips and cover apples with lattice top. Bake for
8 minutes. Reduce oven temperature to 350 degrees and bake
for 30 minutes.

∞ Hershey Bar Pie ∞

1 giant Hershey Bar (plain or
  almond)
1 cup miniature marshmallows

¼ cup milk
1 large carton whipped topping
1 graham cracker pie crust

Combine the Hershey Bar, marshmallows, and milk in a
saucepan. Cook on low heat until smooth, stirring constantly.
Cool. Mix in the whipped topping. Pour mixture into pie crust.
Chill in refrigerator until firm. Garnish with whipped topping
if desired.

∞ Buttermilk Pie ∞

2½ cups sugar
1¼ tablespoons cornstarch
5 eggs, beaten
¾ cup margarine, melted

2 teaspoons vanilla
¾ cup buttermilk
2 unbaked pie shells

Preheat oven to 375 degrees. Mix together the sugar and
cornstarch. Add the eggs and margarine. Add vanilla and
buttermilk. Mix well. Pour in pie shells. Bake until mixture sets,
about 10 minutes. Reduce oven temperature to 325 degrees.
Bake pies for 40 minutes.

WCN Coconut Oatmeal Pie

3 eggs, well beaten
1 cup brown packed sugar
2/3 cup sugar
2/3 cup quick-cooking oats
2/3 cup shredded coconut
1/2 cup milk

2 tablespoons margarine or butter, melted
1 teaspoon vanilla
1/2 cup broken pecans
1 (9-inch) unbaked pie shell

Preheat oven to 450 degrees. Combine the eggs, brown sugar, sugar, oats, coconut, milk, butter, and vanilla in large bowl. Add pecans; mix well. Pour into pie shell. Place pie on broiling trivet in oven. Bake for 8 minutes. Lower temperature to 375 degrees. Bake for 15 minutes or until set.

∞ Chess Pie ∞

1/2 cup margarine
1 1/2 cups sugar
3 eggs, slightly beaten
1 tablespoon cornmeal

1 tablespoon vinegar
1 tablespoon vanilla
1 unbaked pie shell

Preheat oven to 350 degrees. In a saucepan, combine the margarine and sugar. Cook over low heat until smooth. Remove from heat. Add the eggs and cornmeal. Mix well. Add the vinegar and vanilla. Pour the mixture into the pie shell. Bake for 45 minutes.

WCN Pumpkin Chess Pie

1⅓ cups sugar
6 tablespoons butter or margarine, softened
1 cup canned pumpkin
¼ cup plus 2 tablespoons half-and-half
2 eggs
1 teaspoon vanilla
4 teaspoons self-rising cornmeal mix

½ teaspoon salt
½ teaspoon cinnamon
¼ teaspoon ginger
¼ teaspoon nutmeg
¼ teaspoon cloves
1 Press 'n' Bake Cream Cheese Crust
Whipped cream (optional)

Preheat oven to 350 degrees. Cream sugar and butter with electric mixer. Add the pumpkin, half-and-half, eggs, vanilla, cornmeal mix, salt, cinnamon, ginger, nutmeg, and cloves; blend well. Pour mixture into prepared crust. Bake for 40 to 45 minutes or until knife inserted in center comes out clean. Cool on wire rack. Serve chilled and topped with whipped cream.

Press 'n' Bake Cream Cheese Crust:

1 (3-ounce) package cream cheese, at room temperature
½ cup butter or margarine, softened

1 cup sifted flour

Combine cream cheese and butter; blend well. Stir in flour. Refrigerate for 30 minutes. Press dough into bottom and up sides of an 8-inch pie pan. Flute edge as desired. Chill until ready to fill.

∽ Chess Pie II ∾

1/3 cup butter or margarine, melted
1 cup sugar
1/4 cup milk
2 eggs, beaten slightly

1 teaspoon vanilla
1 heaping tablespoon cornmeal
1 tablespoon vinegar
1 unbaked pie shell

Preheat oven to 350 degrees. Combine butter and sugar; mix well. Add milk, eggs, vanilla, cornmeal, and vinegar. Mix well. Pour into pie shell. Bake for about one hour. *This version of chess pie is reduced in fat and sugar. It is not as rich as the usual recipe.*

∽ Chocolate Brownie Pie ∾

2 eggs
1 cup sugar
1/2 cup butter or margarine, melted
1/2 cup flour

1/3 cup cocoa
1/4 teaspoon salt
1/2 cup semisweet chocolate chips
1/2 cup chopped nuts
1 teaspoon vanilla

Preheat oven to 350 degrees. Grease an 8-inch pie pan. Beat eggs in a bowl. Blend in sugar and butter. In a separate bowl stir together flour, cocoa, and salt. Add to egg mixture, beating until blended. Stir in chocolate chips, nuts, and vanilla. Spread in pie pan. Bake for 35 minutes or until set (pie will not test done in center). Cool completely. Serve with ice cream, if desired. *This freezes well and is great to have on hand for unexpected guests.*

❧ Chocolate Chess Tarts ❧

½ cup butter
2 squares unsweetened chocolate
2 eggs
1½ cups sugar

⅓ cup milk
1 tablespoon vanilla
⅛ teaspoon salt
10 unbaked tart shells

Preheat oven to 350 degrees. Melt the butter and chocolate together in saucepan over low heat. Remove from heat; add the sugar. Add the milk, vanilla, and salt; mix well. Pour into tart shells; bake for 25 to 30 minutes.

❧ Pumpkin Pie ❧

3 eggs
2 cups pumpkin
1 can sweetened condensed milk
½ cup brown sugar
½ cup light corn syrup

½ teaspoon salt
1 teaspoon cinnamon
½ teaspoon nutmeg
¼ teaspoon cloves
1 unbaked deep-dish pie shell

Preheat oven to 400 degrees. Beat the eggs thoroughly. Add the pumpkin, sweetened condensed milk, brown sugar, corn syrup, salt, cinnamon, nutmeg, and cloves; mix well. Pour into pie shell. Bake for 50 minutes or until firm.

✧ Impossible Pumpkin Pie ✧

1 cup sugar
1/2 teaspoon salt
1 teaspoon cinnamon
1/2 teaspoon nutmeg
1/2 teaspoon ginger
1/2 teaspoon allspice

1/2 teaspoon cloves
1 (16-ounce) can pumpkin
1 (13-ounce) can evaporated milk
2 eggs
1/2 cup baking mix
1 teaspoon vanilla

Preheat oven to 350 degrees. Combine all ingredients; mix with a mixer for 3 to 4 minutes. Pour into a greased 10-inch pie pan. Bake for 1 hour. *This pie has no crust.*

✧ Pumpkin Chiffon Pie ✧

1 1/4 cups canned pumpkin
2/3 cup milk
1/2 teaspoon salt
1/2 teaspoon nutmeg
1/2 teaspoon ginger
1/2 teaspoon cinnamon
1 cup sugar

3 eggs, separated
1/4 cup cold water
1 tablespoon unflavored gelatin
1 baked pie shell
Whipped cream for garnish
Grated orange rind for garnish

Place the pumpkin, milk, salt, nutmeg, ginger, cinnamon, and 1/2 cup sugar in the top of a double boiler. Heat. Beat the egg yolks slightly. Add the pumpkin mixture to the egg yolks. Return mixture to double boiler; cook until thick. Pour the cold water in a bowl; sprinkle the gelatin on top. Add gelatin to the hot pumpkin mixture. Mix thoroughly. Let cool. When pumpkin mixture begins to stiffen, beat the egg whites until stiff. Beat in the remaining 1/2 cup sugar. Fold whites into the pumpkin mixture. Pour into the pie shell. Chill until firm. Just before serving, garnish with whipped cream and grated orange rind.

✑ Margarita Pie ✑

1 envelope unflavored gelatin
1/4 teaspoon salt
1 cup sugar
4 eggs, separated
1/2 cup lime juice
1 teaspoon grated lime peel

1/4 cup tequila
2 teaspoons orange liqueur
  (optional)
1 (9-inch) baked pie shell
Whipped cream for garnish
Lime slices for garnish

Combine the gelatin, salt, and 1/2 cup of the sugar in a saucepan. Beat together the yolks and lime juice; add to gelatin mixture. Cook over medium heat for 5 to 7 minutes, until gelatin dissolves. Remove from heat. Stir in the lime peel, tequila, and liqueur. Chill until mixture thickens to the consistency of pudding. Beat the egg whites with the remaining 1/2 cup sugar until stiff. Fold into the tequila mixture. Pour into the pie shell. Chill until firm. Garnish with whipped cream and lime slices. Makes 6 to 8 servings.

✑ Margarita Pretzel Pie ✑

1 1/4 cups finely crushed pretzels
1/2 cup plus 2 tablespoons butter,
  softened
1/4 cup sugar
1 (14-ounce) can sweetened
  condensed milk

1/3 cup lime juice
3 or 4 tablespoons tequila
2 tablespoons triple sec
1 cup whipped cream
Additional whipped cream and
  pretzels for garnish

Lightly butter a 9-inch pie plate. Combine the crushed pretzels, butter, and sugar; mix well. Press onto the bottom and sides of the buttered pie plate. In a mixing bowl, combine the sweetened condensed milk, lime juice, tequila, and triple sec. Mix well. Fold in the whipped cream. Freeze for 2 hours or chill for 4 hours. Garnish with whipped cream and pretzels just before serving. *This recipe can be doubled and prepared in a 9-by-11-inch baking pan.*

⌒ French Raisin Pie ⌒

3 eggs, beaten
1/2 cup butter or margarine,
   melted
3/4 cup sugar
1 teaspoon vinegar
1 teaspoon vanilla
1/2 teaspoon cinnamon

1/2 teaspoon allspice
Dash of salt
1/2 cup chopped black walnuts
3/4 cup raisins
1 (8-inch) unbaked pie shell
Whipped cream for topping

Preheat oven to 300 degrees. In a large bowl, combine the eggs, butter, sugar, vinegar, vanilla, cinnamon, allspice, salt, walnuts, and raisins; mix well. Pour into pie shell. Bake for 50 minutes. Serve warm or chilled with whipped cream.

WCN Japanese Fruit Pie

1 cup sugar
1/2 cup margarine, melted
1 egg, beaten
1 teaspoon vanilla

1 tablespoon white vinegar
1/2 cup raisins
1/2 cup coconut
1/2 cup nuts

Preheat oven to 350 degrees. Combine sugar, margarine, eggs, vanilla, and vinegar. Stir in remaining ingredients. Bake for 30 minutes, or until firm.

∽ Caramel Pie ∾

2 cans sweetened condensed milk, unopened

2 graham cracker pie shells
1 carton whipped topping

Place the cans of sweetened condensed milk in a large pot and cover with water. Bring the water to a boil; turn burner to medium heat and cover the pot. Let water boil for 2 hours, adding water to pot as necessary to keep the cans covered. Turn burner off and let cans cool. When cans are completely cool, open them and spread the contents into the pie shells. Cover with whipped topping. Chill until ready to serve.

∽ Peanut Butter Pie ∾

8 ounces cream cheese
1 cup powdered sugar
½ cup peanut butter
½ cup milk

8 ounces whipped topping
1 vanilla wafer or graham cracker pie crust

Combine the cream cheese, powdered sugar, peanut butter, milk, and whipped topping with an electric mixer. Pour into a vanilla wafer or graham cracker crust. Chill until firm.

WCN Peanut Butter Refrigerator Pie

2 (3-ounce) packages cream
  cheese, softened
3/4 cup sifted powdered sugar
1/2 cup crunchy peanut butter
2 1/2 cups whipped topping

1 (8-inch) graham cracker pie
  shell
Coarsely chopped unsalted
  roasted peanuts

Cream the cream cheese and powdered sugar until light and fluffy. Add the peanut butter, beating until smooth and creamy. Fold the whipped topping into the peanut butter mixture. Pour filling into pie shell. Chill 5 to 6 hours or overnight. Garnish with peanuts. Makes 8 servings. *This pie can be frozen and thawed just before serving.*

⚭ Peanut Butter Ice Cream Pie ⚭

1 1/2 cups graham cracker crumbs
1/4 cup sugar
1/2 cup butter or margarine
1 quart vanilla ice cream or
  yogurt

1 1/2 cups chunky peanut butter
1/2 cup whipping cream, whipped
2 tablespoons graham cracker
  crumbs

Combine the 1 1/2 cups graham cracker crumbs, sugar, and butter. Mix well and press into a pie pan. Chill until firm. Place the ice cream in a mixing bowl and stir to soften. Carefully fold in the peanut butter and whipped cream. Quickly spoon the ice cream mixture into the chilled graham cracker crust. Sprinkle the remaining 2 tablespoons graham cracker crumbs around the edge of the pie to garnish. Freeze until firm, about 5 hours. Remove from the freezer 10 to 15 minutes before serving.

WCN Chocolate Chip Pie

2 unbaked pie shells
1 cup broken pecans
1 small package chocolate chips
½ cup margarine, melted

4 eggs, beaten
1 cup sugar
1 cup light corn syrup

Preheat oven to 350 degrees. Divide pecans and chocolate chips in the bottoms of the pie shells. Mix together the margarine, eggs, sugar, and corn syrup; pour into shells. Bake for 30 to 40 minutes.

Derby Pie

1 (9-inch) unbaked pie shell
1 cup chocolate chips
½ cup margarine, melted and
  cooled
1 cup sugar

½ cup flour
2 eggs
1 teaspoon vanilla
¼ teaspoon almond extract
1 cup nuts

Preheat oven to 350 degrees. Spread the chocolate chips over the bottom of the pie shell. Combine the margarine, sugar, flour, eggs, vanilla, almond extract, and nuts. Pour the mixture over the chocolate chips. Bake for 45 minutes.

Derby Pie II

½ cup margarine, melted
1 cup white corn syrup
4 eggs, slightly beaten
1 cup sugar

½ cup chocolate chips
1 cup broken pecans
2 unbaked pie shells

Preheat oven to 350 degrees. Combine the margarine, syrup, eggs, sugar, chocolate chips, and pecans; mix well. Pour into the unbaked pie shells. Bake for about 50 minutes. *If desired, serve with ice cream or whipped topping.*

❧ Chocolate Pie ❧

3 tablespoons cornstarch
Pinch of salt
1½ cups sugar
3 egg yolks
3 tablespoons cocoa
2 cups milk

⅓ stick (almost 3 tablespoons)
  margarine
1 teaspoon vanilla
1 baked pie shell
4 egg whites

Preheat oven to 325 degrees. Combine the cornstarch, salt, and 1 cup of the sugar. Beat the sugar mixture into the egg yolks. Add the cocoa. Add the milk. Cook over medium-low heat until thick. Remove from heat; add the margarine and vanilla. Pour into the pie shell. Beat the egg whites until almost stiff. Add the remaining ½ cup sugar very gradually, one tablespoon at a time, beating after each addition. Beat until stiff. Cover pie with meringue. Bake for 15 to 20 minutes, until golden brown. Keep pie away from drafts until cool.

❧ No-Crust Fudge Pie ❧

1 cup sugar
¼ cup flour
5 tablespoons cocoa
½ cup margarine, melted
2 eggs, beaten

1 teaspoon vanilla
½ cup chopped pecans
Margarine
Vanilla ice cream

Preheat the oven to 325 degrees. Combine the sugar, flour, and cocoa. Add the margarine. Add the eggs; mix well. Stir in the vanilla and pecans. Lightly grease an aluminum pie pan with margarine. Pour the batter into the pie pan. Bake for 27 minutes. Serve warm with vanilla ice cream on top.
Makes 6 servings.

WCN Lemon Meringue Pie

1½ cups sugar
⅓ cup cornstarch
1½ cups water
3 egg yolks, slightly beaten
3 tablespoons butter

¼ cup lemon juice
1 tablespoon grated lemon rind
3 egg whites
1 (9-inch) baked pie shell

Preheat oven to 350 degrees. Combine the sugar and cornstarch in a saucepan. Gradually stir in the water. Cook over medium heat, stirring constantly, until mixture thickens and boils. Boil for 1 minute. Slowly stir at least ½ the hot mixture into the egg yolks; blend egg yolk mixture back into the remaining hot mixture in the saucepan. Boil for 1 minute more, stirring constantly. Remove from heat. Continue stirring until smooth. Blend in the butter, lemon juice, and lemon rind. Pour into the pie shell. Beat the egg whites until peaks form. Cover pie with meringue. Bake until lightly browned.

∽ Strawberry Pie ∽

1 small box strawberry-flavored
   gelatin
4 tablespoons cornstarch
2 cups sugar

2 cups water
1 quart fresh strawberries
2 graham cracker pie shells
Whipped cream to taste

In a saucepan, combine the strawberry-flavored gelatin, cornstarch, sugar, and water. Bring to a boil; boil for 5 minutes. Remove from heat and let cool. While gelatin is cooling, wash, stem, and drain the strawberries. Slice any strawberries that are larger than bite size. Arrange the strawberries in the pie shells. Pour the cooled gelatin over berries until crust is full. Chill for a few hours or overnight. Top with whipped cream and serve.

⬯ French Apple Cobbler ⬯

5 cups peeled, sliced tart apples	1/4 cup water
1 1/4 cups sugar	3 tablespoons margarine, softened
1/2 cup plus 2 tablespoons flour	1 egg, slightly beaten
1/2 teaspoon cinnamon	1/2 teaspoon baking powder
1/2 teaspoon salt	Cream
1 teaspoon vanilla	

Preheat oven to 375 degrees. In a medium bowl, combine the apples, 3/4 cup sugar, 2 tablespoons flour, cinnamon, 1/4 teaspoon salt, vanilla, and water. Turn into a 9-by-9-inch pan. Dot the apples with 1 tablespoon of the margarine. Combine the remaining margarine, egg, baking powder, remaining flour, remaining sugar, and remaining salt. Beat with a wooden spoon until smooth. Drop the batter in 9 portions over the apples, spacing evenly. Batter will spread during baking. Bake for 35 to 40 minutes, or until apples are fork tender and crust is golden brown. Serve warm with cream. Makes 6 to 8 servings. *This cobbler is a delicious change from the standard apple pie.*

⬯ Peach Cobbler ⬯

5 fresh peaches, cut up	1 egg, beaten
5 slices white bread, crust removed	2 tablespoons flour
1 1/2 cups sugar	1/2 cup butter, melted

Preheat oven to 350 degrees. Place the peaches in a 9-by-9-inch casserole dish. Using a rolling pin, roll each slice of bread as thin as possible. Cut each slice into thirds. Place bread strips over peaches. Combine the sugar, egg, flour, and butter. Pour mixture over bread slices. Bake for 35 minutes.

WCN Creamy Lemon Filling

1 (14-ounce) can sweetened
  condensed milk
1 to 2 teaspoons grated lemon
  rind

⅓ cup lemon juice
5 drops yellow food coloring
1½ cups frozen whipped topping,
  thawed

Combine condensed milk, lemon rind, lemon juice, and food coloring; stir well. Fold in whipped topping.

WCN Never-Fail Pie Crust

4 cups flour
1 tablespoon sugar
1 teaspoon baking powder
1 teaspoon salt

1¾ cups shortening
1 cup water
1 teaspoon vinegar
1 egg, well beaten

Blend together flour, sugar, baking powder, salt, and shortening using pastry blender. Add the water, vinegar, and egg. Mix until dough forms a ball. *This will make several flaky crusts and is handy to have on hand in the freezer to bake and use as needed.*

∽ Crunchy Pie Crust ∾

1 cup quick or old-fashioned oats,
  uncooked

¼ cup firmly packed brown sugar
¼ cup margarine, melted

Preheat oven to 350 degrees. Combine all ingredients; mix well. Bake on a baking sheet for 10 minutes, stirring occasionally. Press mixture onto bottom and sides of an 8-inch pie pan. Cool before filling. *Try this easy crust for cream and chiffon pies.*

✺ Peanut Butter Cookies ✺

½ cup butter or margarine
⅓ cup peanut butter
½ cup sugar
½ cup brown sugar

1 egg
1¼ cups self-rising flour
1½ teaspoons vanilla
½ cup chopped peanuts

Preheat oven to 350 degrees. Cream butter and peanut butter. Gradually cream in sugar and brown sugar. Beat in the egg. Stir in the flour, vanilla, and chopped peanuts. Drop by spoonfuls on a greased cookie sheet. Bake for about 12 minutes. Makes about 4 dozen.

✺ Fruitcake Cookies ✺

1 cup bourbon
¾ box seedless raisins
½ cup butter
1 cup brown sugar
4 eggs, unbeaten
2 tablespoons milk
½ pound candied pineapple

½ pound candied cherries
3 cups flour
3 scant teaspoons baking soda
1 teaspoon cloves
1 teaspoon nutmeg
1 teaspoon cinnamon
1½ cups broken pecans

Soak raisins in bourbon overnight. Preheat oven to 275 degrees. Cream butter and brown sugar in a large bowl. Add the eggs one at a time. Add the milk. Combine the candied pineapple and candied cherries. Add 1 cup of the flour to the candied fruit. Sift remaining flour together with the baking soda, cloves, nutmeg, and cinnamon. Add flour mixture to creamed mixture. Add fruit, pecans, raisins, and bourbon to the creamed mixture. Drop by teaspoonfuls on a greased cookie sheet. Bake for 20 to 25 minutes.

❧ Snow Drops ❧

4 tablespoons powdered sugar
2 cups cake flour
7/8 cup butter or margarine
2 teaspoons vanilla

1 teaspoon water
1 cup black walnut meats
Powdered sugar

Preheat oven to 400 degrees. Sift the sugar and flour together. Cut in the butter with a pastry blender. Add the vanilla, water, and walnuts. Press mixture into an 8-by-8-inch pan and cut into rectangles the size of dates. Dip finger in powdered sugar and form rectangles into the shape of a date. Place on greased baking sheet and bake for 10 to 12 minutes. Remove from oven and roll immediately in powdered sugar.

❧ Oatmeal Cookies ❧

1 cup sugar
1 cup vegetable shortening
2 eggs, beaten
1 tablespoon buttermilk
3/4 teaspoon baking soda
2 cups flour

1 teaspoon cinnamon
1/2 teaspoon salt
2 cups oats
1 cup raisins
1 cup nuts

Preheat oven to 350 degrees. Cream sugar and shortening in a mixing bowl. Add eggs. Dissolve baking soda in buttermilk. Add to mixture. Stir in flour, cinnamon, salt, oats, raisins and nuts. Coat a cookie sheet with cooking spray. Drop dough by teaspoons on cookie sheet. Bake for 12 to 15 minutes.

∽ Zasu's Delicious Oatmeal Cookies ∾

1 cup butter
1 cup sugar
1 cup brown sugar
2 teaspoons vanilla
2 eggs
½ teaspoon salt
1 teaspoon baking soda

2¼ cups sifted all-purpose flour
2 tablespoons water
2 cups quick-cooking oats
1 cup seedless raisins
1 cup chopped dates
2 cups chopped nuts

Preheat oven to 375 degrees. Cream butter, sugar, brown sugar, and vanilla. Mix well. Add eggs; beat thoroughly. Add baking soda and salt to flour. Add to sugar mixture. Add water, oats, raisins, dates, and nuts. Blend well. Drop by spoonfuls on a cookie sheet and bake for about 8 or 9 minutes.

∽ Scottish Shortbread ∾

1 cup butter
¼ cup sugar

2 teaspoons vanilla
2½ cups unsifted flour

Preheat oven to 350 degrees. Cream butter and sugar. Add vanilla. Gradually add flour. When dough holds together, form fingers about 2 inches long, ½ inch wide, and ½ inch thick. Bake for 15 minutes.

☙ Brown Sugar Brownies ❧

1 cup margarine
1 box dark brown sugar
4 eggs, beaten
2 scant cups flour
1 teaspoon baking powder

Dash of salt
2 teaspoons vanilla
1 cup chopped pecans
Glaze

Do not preheat oven. Melt margarine and brown sugar together. Beat in eggs. Add the flour, baking powder, salt, vanilla, and pecans. Mix well. Pour into a greased 9-by-13-inch pan. Bake in an un-preheated oven at 300 degrees for 35 minutes. Cool and glaze. *These taste best when left standing overnight.*

Glaze:

1 cup light brown sugar
2 tablespoons milk
2 tablespoons margarine

1 tablespoon flour
Dash of salt
1 teaspoon vanilla

Combine ingredients in a medium saucepan. Bring to a boil; boil for one minute. Pour over brownies.

☙ Chess Cake Cookies ❧

1 (18-ounce) package lemon
  supreme cake mix
½ cup butter
3 large eggs
2 (8-ounce) packages cream
  cheese, cut in chunks

½ cup sugar
½ teaspoon vanilla
2 teaspoons lemon juice

Preheat oven to 350 degrees. Grease and flour a 9-by-13-inch pan. Mix cake mix, butter, and 1 egg until crumbly. Press into pan. Bake for 8 minutes. Beat cream cheese in medium bowl until fluffy. Mix in the 2 remaining eggs, sugar, vanilla, and lemon juice. Pour over hot crust. Bake for 25 minutes.

ᗉ Cranberry Crunch Bars ᗉ

1³/4 cups sifted flour
³/4 teaspoon salt
1¹/2 teaspoons cinnamon
1¹/4 cups brown sugar
2 cups quick rolled oats
1 cup butter or margarine
1 cup finely chopped walnuts

¹/2 cup sugar
2 heaping tablespoons cornstarch
2 jars Ocean Spray orange-
   cranberry relish
1 egg
1 tablespoon water
Powdered sugar

Preheat oven to 400 degrees. Sift flour, salt, and cinnamon in large bowl. Stir in brown sugar and oats. Cut in butter until mixture is crumbly. Stir in walnuts. Press half of mixture into the bottom of a greased 9-by-13-inch pan. Pat evenly. Bake for 5 minutes. Cool slightly. Reduce oven temperature to 375 degrees. While layer bakes, mix sugar and cornstarch in a medium saucepan. Stir in relish and heat to boiling, stirring constantly until thick. Boil for 3 minutes; remove from heat. Spread evenly over layer in pan. Sprinkle remaining oat mixture over the top. Pat evenly and press firmly. Beat egg well in a cup. Stir in the water. Brush egg mixture lightly over top of crumb mixture. Bake for 30 minutes. Cool completely. Cut into bars. Dust lightly with powdered sugar. Makes 4 dozen. *To make 8 dozen bars, double all ingredients except the relish.*

ᗉ Date Skillet Cookies ᗉ

2 eggs
1 cup sugar
¹/2 cup margarine
1 (8-ounce) box chopped dates
2 cups crispy rice cereal

¹/2 cup chopped pecans
¹/2 cup coconut
1 teaspoon vanilla
Coconut for coating

Combine the eggs, sugar, margarine, and dates in a skillet. Bring to a boil; boil for 5 to 8 minutes over medium heat. Remove from heat. Stir in crispy rice cereal, pecans, and coconut. Add vanilla. Let cool. Form into balls and roll in coconut.

∽ Orange Coconut Balls ∾

1 (16-ounce) package vanilla
  wafers, crushed
1 cup powdered sugar
Nuts (optional)
½ cup butter or margarine

1 (6-ounce) can frozen orange
  juice, thawed and undiluted
1 (6-ounce) package frozen
  coconut

Combine vanilla wafers, sugar, nuts (if desired), margarine, and orange juice. Stir well. Shape into 1-inch balls. Roll in coconut. Chill until firm. Makes 3 dozen. *These may be frozen on a cookie sheet and stored in freezer bags or containers. Allow them to thaw in the refrigerator before serving.*

∽ Graham Cracker Toffee Bars ∾

About 12 graham cracker squares,
  whole, not crushed
1 cup brown sugar
1 cup butter or margarine

1 cup chopped pecans
1 (12-ounce) package chocolate
  chips

Preheat oven to 350 degrees. Line a 9-by-12-inch pan with graham crackers. In a saucepan combine the brown sugar, butter, and pecans. Bring to a rolling boil; boil for 5 minutes. Pour over graham crackers. Bake for 10 minutes. Remove from oven. Pour chocolate chips over toffee and allow them to melt. Spread melted chocolate evenly over the top. Let cool. Cut into bars.

WCN Delicious Brownies

2 cups sugar
1/2 cup margarine, melted
4 eggs
1 1/2 cups flour (plain)

1/4 teaspoon salt
1/2 cup cocoa
2 teaspoons vanilla
Nuts, as desired

Preheat oven to 325. Beat sugar into margarine; beat in eggs, flour, salt, and cocoa. Add the sugar mixture. Add the vanilla and nuts. Pour into a 9-by-13-inch pan. Bake for 30 minutes.

WCN Butterscotch Bars

1 1/2 cups margarine, cut in pieces
2 cups brown sugar
3 teaspoons vanilla
3 eggs

3 cups flour
3 teaspoons baking powder
1 1/2 teaspoons salt
1 1/2 cups walnuts, broken pieces

Preheat oven to 350 degrees. Cream together margarine, sugar, and vanilla. Add eggs to sugar mixture. Add flour, baking powder, and salt. Mix well. Add walnuts. Bake for 30 to 40 minutes or until light brown.

WCN Hello Dollys

1/2 cup butter
1 cup graham cracker crumbs
1 cup coconut
1 cup chocolate chips

1 cup caramel chips
1 cup nuts
1 can sweetened condensed milk

Preheat oven to 350 degrees. Melt butter in a glass 9-by-9-inch baking dish. Sprinkle the graham cracker crumbs over the butter. Sprinkle the coconut over the crumbs. Sprinkle the chocolate chips and caramel chips over the coconut. Add the nuts. Pour the sweetened condensed milk over the mixture. Bake for 30 minutes. Cut into squares.

∽ Chess Cake Squares ∾

1 package lemon supreme cake
  mix
1/2 cup butter
3 large eggs
2 (8-ounce) packages cream
  cheese, cut in chunks

1/2 cup sugar
1/2 teaspoon vanilla
2 teaspoons lemon juice

Preheat oven to 350 degrees. Grease and flour a 9-by-13-inch pan. Mix together the cake mix, butter, and 1 egg until crumbly. Press into pan. Bake for 8 minutes. In a medium bowl beat the cream cheese until fluffy. Mix in the 2 eggs, sugar, vanilla, and lemon juice. Pour over hot crust. Bake for 25 minutes.

∽ Butterscotch Delight ∾

1 1/2 cups all-purpose flour
1/2 cup plus 2 tablespoons butter
  or margarine
1/2 cup chopped pecans
1 (8-ounce) package cream cheese
1 cup powdered sugar
1 (8-ounce) carton whipped
  topping

2 packages butterscotch
  pudding mix
1 teaspoon brown sugar
2 3/4 cups milk
1 teaspoon vanilla
Chopped nuts to taste

Preheat oven to 375 degrees. Mix together the flour, butter, and pecans; press into the bottom of a 9-by-13-inch pan. Bake for 20 minutes or until lightly browned. Let cool. Mix together the cream cheese, sugar, and 1/2 of the whipped topping. Spread on cooled crust. In a saucepan, combine the pudding mix, brown sugar, and milk. Cook until thick. Add the vanilla. Let pudding mixture cool. Spread the cooled pudding over the cream cheese layer. Top with the remaining whipped topping. Sprinkle with chopped nuts. Chill for 2 hours; cut into squares. Makes 15 servings.

❧ The State Cookie of Tennessee ❧

¼ **cup butter, softened**
¼ **cup margarine, softened**
½ **cup dark brown sugar**
½ **cup sugar**
1 **large egg**
1 **tablespoon milk**
1 **teaspoon vanilla**
1 **cup flour**

½ **teaspoon baking powder**
½ **teaspoon baking soda**
½ **teaspoon salt**
1¼ **cups 3-Minute brand quick oats (they're already toasted)**
¾ **cup raisins**
¾ **cup chopped English walnuts, toasted**

In a large mixer bowl cream the butter, margarine, brown sugar, and sugar. Add the egg, milk, and vanilla; beat until light and fluffy. In a medium bowl, stir together the flour, baking powder, baking soda, salt, and oats. Add to creamed mixture and mix until blended. Stir in the raisins and walnuts. Cover and refrigerate for at least 1 hour. Preheat oven to 350 degrees. Line Tennessee-shaped cookie pan with aluminum foil. Spread cookie dough over whole pan, pressing to flatten. Bake for 20 to 25 minutes. (The top of the cookie will be slightly soft and moist but will finish baking while still in the pan.) Allow to set in the pan for 10 to 15 minutes. Remove from pan, lifting out with help of foil. Remove to wire rack to cool completely. Decorate as desired. Makes one Tennessee cookie. *To toast walnuts, place on a microwave-safe dish and heat on high for 4 to 5 minutes, stirring every minute; or toast in 350-degree oven for 10 to 15 minutes. For thinner cookies, divide cookie dough in half; bake for 12 to 16 minutes.*

∽ No-Bake Chocolate Oatmeal Cookies ∽

2 cups sugar
½ cup cocoa
½ cup milk
½ cup butter

½ cup peanut butter
1 teaspoon vanilla
3 cups oats

In a saucepan mix together the sugar, cocoa, and milk. Bring to a boil; boil for one minute. Remove from heat. Add the butter, peanut butter, vanilla, and oats. Mix well. Drop on waxed paper or aluminum foil. Let cool. *Use crunchy peanut butter or add pecans to vary the recipe.*

WCN Basic Sugar Cookies

⅔ cup vegetable shortening
¾ cup sugar
1 teaspoon vanilla
1 egg

4 teaspoons milk
2 cups sifted flour
1½ teaspoons baking powder
¼ teaspoon salt

Preheat oven to 375 degrees. Cream shortening, sugar, and vanilla. Add egg and milk; beat until light and fluffy. Sift together flour, baking powder, and salt; blend into creamed mixture. Divide dough in half; cover and chill for at least 1 hour. Roll half of dough to ⅛-inch thickness on a lightly floured surface. Chill other half until ready to use. Cut into desired shapes with cutters. Bake on ungreased cookie sheet for 8 to 10 minutes. Cool slightly; remove from pan. Makes 3 dozen cookies.

WCN Vanilla Sugar Cookies

1 cup margarine, softened	4 cups flour
1 cup vegetable oil	1 teaspoon cream of tartar
1 cup sugar	1 teaspoon baking soda
1 cup powdered sugar	1/4 teaspoon salt
2 eggs	4 teaspoons vanilla

Preheat oven to 350 degrees. Cream the margarine, oil, sugar, and powdered sugar. Add the eggs one at a time, beating after each addition. Add the flour, cream of tartar, baking soda, salt, and vanilla. Beat well with a mixer. Chill for at least 1 hour. Form small balls of chilled dough; roll in granulated sugar. Place on cookie sheet and flatten with fork. Bake for 10 minutes.

WCN Tea Cakes

1 cup butter or margarine, softened	5 cups flour
2 cups sugar	1 teaspoon baking soda
3 eggs	1 teaspoon vanilla
2 tablespoons buttermilk	Sugar for sprinkling

Preheat oven to 400 degrees. Cream the butter; gradually add sugar, beating well. Add the eggs one at a time, beating after each addition. Add the buttermilk and beat well. Combine the flour and baking soda; gradually stir into creamed mixture. Stir in vanilla. Chill dough several hours or overnight. Roll out dough to 1/4-inch thickness on a lightly floured surface. Cut into rounds with a 3 1/2-inch cookie cutter. Place 1 inch apart on a lightly greased cookie sheet; sprinkle with sugar. Bake for 7 to 8 minutes or until edges are lightly browned. Remove cookies to wire rack. Let cool completely. Makes 4 dozen.

WCN Chocolate Chip Cookies

5 cups old-fashioned oats, uncooked
2 cups butter, softened
2 cups packed brown sugar
2 cups sugar
4 large eggs
2 tablespoons vanilla
4 cups all-purpose flour
1 teaspoon salt
2 teaspoons baking powder
2 teaspoons baking soda
2 (12-ounce) packages semisweet chocolate pieces
1 (8-ounce) milk chocolate bar, grated
3 cups chopped walnuts (optional)

Preheat oven to 350 degrees. Blend oats to a fine powder in the blender. Cream butter, sugar, and brown sugar with a mixer in a large bowl until light and fluffy. Beat in eggs and vanilla. In another bowl, combine the oatmeal powder, flour, salt, baking powder, and baking soda. Add oat mixture to butter mixture; beat just until blended. With a wooden spoon, stir in chocolate pieces, grated chocolate, and nuts. Roll dough by rounded tablespoon into balls; place 2 inches apart on ungreased cookie sheet. Bake 12 to 15 minutes or until golden brown.

WCN Oatmeal-Raisin Cookies

1 cup all-purpose flour
1/2 teaspoon baking powder
1/4 teaspoon baking soda
1/2 teaspoon salt
1/3 cup sugar
1/3 teaspoon cinnamon
1 cup regular oats, uncooked
1/2 cup raisins
1/3 cup vegetable oil
1/4 cup egg substitute
1/4 cup water

Preheat oven to 400 degrees. Combine the flour, baking powder, soda, salt, sugar, cinnamon, oats, and raisins in a large mixing bowl; stir well. Add remaining ingredients; stir well. Drop dough by teaspoonfuls onto an ungreased non-stick cookie sheet. Bake for 8 to 10 minutes or until done.
Makes 3 1/2 dozen cookies.

∞ Brandied Orange Custard ∞

8 large navel oranges
1⅓ cups sugar
2 tablespoons cognac (brandy)
2 envelopes unflavored gelatin

½ cup cold water
1½ cups heavy cream
Grated unsweetened chocolate

Cut stems off oranges. Using a zigzag pattern, cut oranges in half. Hollow out the inside of the oranges and place in shallow dish. Mash pulp to make 3 cups juice. Stir sugar and cognac into juice until sugar dissolves. Sprinkle gelatin over cold water in double boiler. Simmer until gelatin dissolves. Pour in separate bowl. Slowly stir juice into dissolved gelatin. Add ¾ cup heavy cream and stir. Place in orange shells and chill until firm. Whip remaining cream and place on top. Grate chocolate over the top and serve.

∞ Danish Pudding ∞

1 cup butter
1¾ cups sugar
3 eggs
1 cup buttermilk
1½ teaspoons baking soda
1 small package dates
1 cup chopped pecans

3 cups flour
1 teaspoon salt
1 tablespoon orange juice
1¼ cups orange juice
1 cup sugar
Grated rind of one orange

Preheat oven to 350 degrees. Cream butter and sugar. Add eggs. Dissolve soda in buttermilk. Coat the dates and pecans with a small amount of flour. Set aside. Mix salt and remaining flour together. Add the buttermilk mixture and flour mixture alternately to the creamed mixture. Stir well after each addition. Stir in the dates and pecans. Add 1 tablespoon orange juice. Bake in a tube pan for 1 hour. Mix 1¼ cups orange juice with 1 cup sugar and the grated rind of 1 orange; let stand while cake is baking. Pour juice mixture over the cake as soon as it comes from the oven or while the cake is still warm.

∾ Old-Fashioned Boiled Custard ∾

3 large eggs	1 tablespoon vanilla
4 cups whole milk	Nutmeg (optional)
⅔ cup sugar	Whipped cream

Beat the eggs well. Be sure to remove the small membrane connecting the white and yolk of each egg so you won't have bits of cooked egg white in your custard. Combine the milk, eggs, and sugar. Cook over boiling water in a double boiler, stirring constantly, until custard "coats" the back of the spoon. Remove from heat and let cool to room temperature. Add vanilla. Refrigerate. Serve cold with a dusting of nutmeg and whipped cream as topping.

∾ Pecan Puffs ∾

½ cup butter, room temperature	1 teaspoon vanilla
2 tablespoons sugar	1 cup crushed pecans
1 cup cake flour, sifted twice	1 box powdered sugar

Cream butter and sugar in mixer until creamy. Add flour and vanilla slowly, mixing well. Add crushed pecans; mix well. It is easier to add the pecans with a spoon. It helps to refrigerate this mixture for an hour or overnight. Preheat the oven to 300 degrees. Grease a cookie sheet with butter. (I save the butter wrapper to grease the pan.) Roll the dough into balls the size of a nickel. Bake on the middle or top rack or until light tan in color. Watch constantly after puffs have baked for 15 to 20 minutes. Cool until cold and roll in sifted powdered sugar. Store in an airtight can. Can be kept for months. *If desired, use this substitute for cake flour: sift 2 rounded tablespoons of cornstarch into a 1-cup measure; fill the cup with sifted all-purpose flour.*

∽ Butterhorns ∾

1 cup sour cream	Melted margarine
2 cups flour	Ground nuts
½ pound margarine, softened	Brown sugar
Cinnamon	Icing

Combine the sour cream, flour, and margarine. Mix well. Refrigerate for 2 hours. Preheat oven to 400 degrees. Cut dough into 4 parts. Roll one part into a circle. Sprinkle cinnamon, melted margarine, ground nuts, and brown sugar (easy on brown sugar) onto circle. Grease pan well. Cut circle into twelve parts (like pie). Roll corner to corner, starting with a large end. Place open end down. Bake for 15 minutes. Drizzle with icing. Repeat process for rest of dough.

Icing:

2 tablespoons milk	½ teaspoon vanilla
1 cup powdered sugar	

Combine ingredients, stirring well.

∽ Strawberry Parfait ∾

1 can sweetened condensed milk	1 (10-ounce) package frozen
⅓ cup lemon juice	strawberries (or 1 pint fresh
1 (8-ounce) carton sour cream	strawberries, crushed)

Combine ingredients. Spoon into parfait glasses and chill. Before serving place a spoonful of whipped cream or frozen whipped topping on each parfait and top with a strawberry or maraschino cherry.

WCN Banana Pudding

1 cup sugar	24 vanilla wafers
1/4 cup cornstarch	3 large ripe bananas, sliced
1/4 teaspoon salt	3 egg whites, at room temperature
2 cups milk	1/4 teaspoon cream of tartar
3 egg yolks	1/4 cup plus 2 tablespoons sugar
2 tablespoons butter or margarine	1/2 teaspoon vanilla
1 teaspoon vanilla	

Preheat oven to 350 degrees. Combine the sugar, cornstarch, and salt in the top of a double boiler. Stir in the milk; bring water to a boil. Reduce heat to low; cook, stirring constantly, for 10 to 12 minutes or until slightly thickened. Beat egg yolks until thick and lemon colored. Gradually stir about 1/4 of the hot mixture into yolks; blend the yolk mixture back into the remaining hot mixture, stirring constantly. Cook, stirring constantly, until mixture thickens. Remove from heat. Gently stir in the butter and 1 teaspoon vanilla. Layer 1/2 of the vanilla wafers in a 2 1/2-quart baking dish; top with 1/2 of the bananas. Pour 1/2 of the filling over the bananas. Repeat layers. Combine the egg whites and cream of tartar; beat until foamy. Gradually add 1/4 cup plus 2 tablespoons sugar, 1 tablespoon at a time, beating until stiff peaks form. Beat in the remaining 1/2 teaspoon vanilla. Spread meringue over filling, sealing to edge of dish. Bake for 10 to 12 minutes or until golden brown.

∞ Bananas Foster ∞

2 tablespoons brown sugar	Dash cinnamon
1 tablespoon butter	½ ounce banana liqueur
1 ripe banana, peeled, sliced lengthwise	1 ounce white rum
	1 large scoop vanilla ice cream

Melt the brown sugar and butter in a flat chafing dish. Add the banana and sauté until tender. Sprinkle with cinnamon. Pour the banana liqueur and rum over the banana. Inflame. Baste with warm liqueur until flame burns out. Serve over ice cream. Makes 1 large serving.

∞ "Death by Chocolate" Truffle ∞

1 (large) box fudge brownie mix	6 toffee candy bars
4 tablespoons coffee	1 (12-ounce) carton whipped topping
2 or 3 boxes chocolate mousse mix, or homemade Chocolate Mousse (following page)	

Bake brownies according to package directions for cake brownies. Cool. Use a fork to punch holes all over the brownies. Pour coffee over brownies. Set aside. Whip up the chocolate mousse according to package directions. Break toffee candy bars into small pieces using a food processor or a hammer. Cover the brownies with ½ of the mousse. Sprinkle with ½ of the candy pieces. Spread ½ of the whipped topping over the candy. Repeat layers with remaining ingredients. Refrigerate! *Chocolate mousse mix can be difficult to find. If desired, use the following recipe to make your own mousse. It is also great in a prepared chocolate pie shell topped with whipped topping and chocolate curls!*

෨ Chocolate Mousse ෨

1 cup semisweet chocolate pieces
1 egg
2 eggs, separated

1 teaspoon vanilla
2 cups whipped topping

Melt chocolate pieces in a double boiler over hot, but not boiling, water. Remove from heat and cool slightly. With a hand mixer beat in the egg and 2 egg yolks one at a time; add the vanilla. In a small bowl, with mixer at high speed, beat the 2 egg whites until soft peaks form. Fold the egg whites into the chocolate mixture. Using a wire whisk, gently fold in the whipped topping.

෨ Layered Lemon Gelatin ෨

1 package lemon-flavored gelatin
3/4 cup butter or margarine
3/4 cup sugar
1 egg, separated
1 cup chopped nuts

1 cup crushed pineapple, drained
1 box vanilla wafers
Whipped topping and cherries for
  garnish

Prepare the lemon-flavored gelatin as directed on the box; set aside. Cream together the butter and sugar. Beat the egg yolk; add to butter mixture. Add the nuts and pineapple. Beat the egg white; fold into pineapple mixture. Put a layer of vanilla wafers in a greased pan. Follow with 1/2 of the pineapple mixture. Repeat vanilla wafer and pineapple layers. Top with a layer of vanilla wafers. Pour the partially set gelatin mixture over the vanilla wafers. Chill until firm. Serve with whipped topping and cherries.

⤸ Orange Crush Sherbet ⤸

2 (28-ounce) bottles of orange-
flavored soda
2 (14-ounce) cans sweetened
condensed milk

1 (16-ounce) can crushed
pineapple

Combine all ingredients in a bowl; mix well. Pour into an ice cream freezer container. Freeze according to manufacturer's instructions. Makes 16 servings. *This recipe makes great homemade sherbet that is also very low in fat.*

⤸ Watkins Country-Style Vanilla Ice Cream ⤸

4 eggs
2½ cups sugar
4 cups whipping cream

2 tablespoons vanilla
¼ teaspoon salt
5 cups milk (approximate)

In a large mixing bowl, beat eggs until foamy. Gradually add sugar; beat until thickened. Add the cream, vanilla, and salt; mix thoroughly. Pour into ice cream freezer container; add milk up to line on can. Stir well. Freeze according to manufacturer's instructions. Makes 4 quarts.

⤳ Peanut Butter Fudge ⤵

3 cups sugar
1 cup milk
2 tablespoons light corn syrup

Pinch salt
2 tablespoons butter
1 cup peanut butter

Combine the sugar, milk, corn syrup, and salt in a saucepan. Bring to a boil. Boil to soft ball stage. Add 2 tablespoons butter and 1 cup peanut butter. Beat and pour into 8-by-8-inch baking dish. Let cool and then cut into squares.

⤳ Toffee Bars ⤵

1 cup butter or margarine
1 cup brown sugar
1 teaspoon vanilla
2 cups sifted enriched flour

1 (6-ounce) package semisweet
  chocolate pieces
1 cup chopped California walnuts

Preheat oven to 350 degrees. Thoroughly cream together the butter, brown sugar, and vanilla. Add flour; mix well. Stir in the chocolate pieces and walnuts. Press mixture into an ungreased $15^1/_2$-by-$10^1/_2$-by-1-inch jelly roll pan. Bake for 25 minutes or until brown. Cut into bars or squares while still warm. Let cool before removing from pan. Makes 4 dozen.

WCN Bourbon Balls

1 cup vanilla wafer crumbs
1 cup chopped pecans
1 cup powdered sugar

2 tablespoons cocoa
3 ounces bourbon
$1^1/_2$ tablespoons light corn syrup

Mix together the vanilla wafer crumbs, pecans, sugar, cocoa, and bourbon. Add the corn syrup and mix well. Form into balls and roll in additional powdered sugar. Chill well.
Makes about 40 pieces.

∽ Microwave Peanut Brittle ∾

1 cup sugar
½ cup light or dark corn syrup
1 cup peanuts (or pecans, if desired)

1 teaspoon margarine
1 teaspoon vanilla
1 teaspoon baking soda

Mix sugar, syrup, and nuts in a microwavable bowl. Microwave on High for 4 minutes. Remove and stir with wooden spoon. Microwave on High for 4 minutes longer. Remove from oven and stir again. Add margarine and vanilla. Microwave on High for 1 minute. Remove from oven and stir in baking soda until mixture is light and fluffy (this does not take long.) Pour out onto a greased cookie sheet and let cool. Break into pieces. Makes about 1¼ pounds.

∽ Confection Bites ∾

¾ cup butter, softened
4 tablespoons sugar
2 cups flour
1 cup chopped pecans

2 teaspoons vanilla
1 tablespoon milk
Powdered sugar

Cream the butter and sugar. Work in the flour and pecans. Add milk very gradually—practically drop by drop. Add the vanilla. Chill until cool. Preheat oven to 400 degrees. Form flour mixture into small rolls or balls. Bake for about 12 minutes or until crisp and lightly brown. Remove from oven; roll immediately in powdered sugar. Makes about 3 dozen.

⊙ Heath Bar Candy ⊙

1 cup butter	1 tablespoon water
1⅓ cups sugar	1½ cups finely chopped pecans
1 tablespoon corn syrup	3 chocolate bars

Melt the butter in a saucepan; add the sugar, corn syrup, and water. Cook and stir until a candy thermometer registers 300 degrees (hard ball stage). Quickly remove from heat and stir in 1 cup pecans. Spread in a well-greased 9-by-13-inch pan. Let cool for 15 minutes. Turn syrup mixture onto waxed paper. Melt the chocolate bars over low heat; spread on top of syrup mixture. Sprinkle with the remaining 1/2 cup pecans. Chill until firm and cool. Break into pieces of desired size.

⊙ Pralines ⊙

3 cups (1 box) light brown sugar	¼ teaspoon salt
1 cup heavy cream	1 teaspoon vanilla
¼ cup butter	1½ cups pecan halves
2 tablespoons light corn syrup	

In a heavy saucepan combine the brown sugar, cream, butter, corn syrup, and salt. Bring to a boil; boil, stirring occasionally, until candy thermometer registers 234 degrees (soft ball stage). Remove from heat; let cool for 5 minutes. Stir in the vanilla and pecans. Beat with a spoon until the mixture begins to thicken and lose its gloss. Drop by spoonfuls onto waxed paper. Spread to form patties.

∽ Divinity ∾

2½ cups sugar
½ cup water
½ cup light corn syrup

2 egg whites, at room temperature
1 teaspoon vanilla
1 cup chopped pecans

Combine the sugar, water, and corn syrup in a 3-quart saucepan. Cook over low heat, stirring gently, until sugar dissolves. Cover and cook over medium heat for 2 to 3 minutes until sugar crystals are washed down from the sides of the pan. Uncover and cook over medium heat without stirring to hard ball stage, or to 260 degrees on a candy thermometer. Remove from heat. Beat the egg whites in a large mixing bowl until stiff peaks form. Pour the hot sugar mixture in a very thin stream over egg whites while beating constantly at high speed with an electric mixer. Add the vanilla and continue beating just until mixture holds its shape. Stir in the pecans. Drop by rounded teaspoonfuls onto waxed paper. Let cool.

∽ Crystallized Pecans ∾

1½ cups sugar
½ cup water
2 cups pecans

2 tablespoons orange juice
Grated rind of 2 oranges

In a small saucepan combine the sugar and water. Heat, stirring, until mixture comes to a boil. Cook mixture without stirring until the syrup reaches soft ball stage, or to 240 degrees on a candy thermometer. Remove pan from heat. Stir in the pecans, orange juice, and grated rind. Continue to stir the syrup until it is cloudy and begins to look grainy. Spread nuts on waxed paper to cool and harden. Break apart in pieces as desired.

∞ Peanut Butter Balls ∞

1 cup margarine
1½ boxes powdered sugar
3 cups crunchy peanut butter
2½ cups crispy rice cereal

1 rectangle paraffin wax
1 (12-ounce) package chocolate
  chips

In a large pan over low heat combine the margarine, powdered sugar, peanut butter, and crispy rice cereal; mix well. Remove from heat; chill. In a saucepan, melt together the paraffin wax and chocolate chips. Form the chilled peanut butter mixture into balls and dip into melted chocolate. Place on waxed paper to cool.

WCN Peanut Butter Cups

1 cup crunchy peanut butter
1 cup butter
2 cups powdered sugar
2 cups graham cracker crumbs

1½ cups milk chocolate chips
4 tablespoons peanut butter
  (crunchy)

Combine the 1 cup peanut butter and butter in a saucepan. Melt over low heat. Remove from heat. Add the powdered sugar and graham cracker crumbs. Press the mixture into a 9-by-13-inch pan. Refrigerate until cool. In a saucepan over low heat, melt the milk chocolate chips and 4 tablespoons peanut butter. Spread over the mixture; let cool. Cut or break into pieces.

Extras

Sauces, Spreads, Dressings & Pickles

End of the Season Pickle

2 quarts green tomatoes	3 red sweet peppers
1 quart red tomatoes	3 bunches celery
3 green sweet peppers	3 large onions
	1 small head cabbage
	1/2 cup salt

Chop vegetables, cover with salt, let stand over night. In the morning drain well, add 2 lbs. of brown sugar and 3 pints of vinegar; one teaspoon each mustard and black pepper. Cook until it boils 3 minutes. Seal.

Mrs. Percy Myatt

Recipe from WCN Cookbook of 1922

∽ Marinade for Pork Tenderloin ∾

1 (12-ounce) can beer
½ cup orange marmalade
¼ cup sugar

½ cup soy sauce
2 cloves garlic, minced

Combine ingredients and pour over pork tenderloin. Marinate, refrigerated, for up to 10 hours. Grill tenderloin for about 30 minutes or until done. Serve with Jezebel Sauce.

∽ Jezebel Sauce for Pork Tenderloin ∾

1 (10-ounce) jar orange
  marmalade
1 small jar Coleman's or Creole
  prepared mustard

1 (10-ounce) jar apple jelly
1 small jar horseradish
Salt and pepper to taste

Combine ingredients and mix well. Serve with pork tenderloin.

∽ Barbecue Sauce ∾

2 cups catsup
¾ cup cider vinegar
¼ cup mustard
½ tablespoon black pepper

3 cups water
1½ tablespoons chili powder
1 tablespoon Worcestershire sauce

Combine all ingredients in a saucepan; stir with a wire whisk until thoroughly mixed. Bring to boil. Simmer, uncovered, stirring frequently, for about an hour, until sauce has cooked down to 1 pint. *This sauce will keep in the refrigerator for quite a while.*

WCN Vanilla Sauce

²/₃ cup sugar
1 tablespoon cornstarch
Dash of salt
1 cup boiling water

1 tablespoon butter
1 teaspoon vanilla
1 tablespoon cream sherry

Mix sugar, cornstarch, and salt. Add to boiling water. Cook until mixture is clear and thickens. Remove from heat; add butter, vanilla, and sherry.

Pimento Cheese

1 (8-ounce) package Cheddar
  cheese, shredded
1 (8-ounce) package sharp
  Cheddar cheese, shredded
1 (8-ounce) package Velveeta
  cheese, shredded

1½ tablespoons sugar
¼ teaspoon salt
¼ teaspoon pepper
1 (4-ounce) jar diced pimentos
1 cup mayonnaise

Combine all ingredients. Mix well. Makes 1 quart. *This sandwich filling may be frozen for later use.*

Frozen Strawberry Preserves

2 cups crushed strawberries
4 cups sugar

¾ cup water
1 box Sure-Jell

Mix strawberries with sugar. Combine the water and Sure-Jell in a saucepan. Bring to a boil; boil for 1 minute, stirring constantly. Pour over sugared berries. Cook, stirring constantly, for 3 minutes. Pour into jars and cover with lids. Let stand at room temperature, tightly covered, for 24 hours before storing in freezer.

∽ Cranberry Jam ∾

1 package cranberries
1 large can crushed pineapple
2 cups sugar
Juice and peel (white membrane removed) of 1 orange, cut in small pieces

Juice and zest of 1 lemon
1 cup chopped nuts
½ teaspoon cinnamon
¼ teaspoon cloves

Combine ingredients in a large pot. Cook until thickened, 10 to 15 minutes. Pour into hot jelly jars and seal.

∽ Holiday Jam ∾

1 pound dried apricots, finely chopped
6 cups water
1 (16-ounce) can crushed pineapple

6 cups sugar
¼ cup maraschino cherries, finely chopped

Soak the apricots in water for 12 hours. Add the pineapple and bring to a boil over medium heat. Boil for 20 minutes. Add the sugar and cherries. Boil for 10 minutes. Test to see if mixture is set. Put in jars and cover. *Jars of this jam make nice holiday gifts.*

WCN Sweet-Sour French Dressing

1 cup vegetable oil
½ cup vinegar
1 cup catsup
½ cup plus 2 teaspoons sugar
2 teaspoons paprika

2 teaspoons salt
¼ teaspoon black pepper
¼ teaspoon garlic powder
¼ celery seed

Combine all ingredients; blend well. Chill for several hours.
Makes 2½ cups.

WCN Curry French Dressing

3 cups vinegar
6 cups oil
3 teaspoons curry powder
½ cup catsup

3 teaspoons salt
¾ cup sugar
2 cups onion, finely chopped
3 teaspoons paprika

Combine all ingredients; blend well. Chill for several hours.

∽ Salad Dressing for Fruit ∽

1 cup sugar
1 heaping tablespoon flour
Pinch salt
2 egg yolks
1 heaping tablespoon butter

Juice of 1 lemon
1 small (6-ounce) can crushed
   pineapple
Fruit of choice

Combine ingredients. Cook over medium heat until thick and
clear. Remove from heat and let cool. Pour over your favorite
fruit and mix well.

∞ Blueberry Poppy Seed Dressing ∞

¼ cup fresh blueberries	2 cups mayonnaise
¼ cup white vinegar	2 tablespoons poppy seeds
⅓ cup brown sugar	

Purée the blueberries and vinegar in a blender. Pour the purée into a saucepan over low heat. Add brown sugar. Cook, stirring, until brown sugar is dissolved. Remove from heat. Let cool. Combine cooled mixture, mayonnaise, and poppy seeds in blender. Refrigerate. Makes approximately 2¹/₂ cups.

∞ Holiday Relish ∞

1 pound whole cranberries	2 oranges, peeled, seeded, and finely chopped
2 large apples, unpeeled, finely chopped	Rind from one orange, grated
2 ripe pears, unpeeled, chopped	1 cup pecans, chopped (optional)
1 (8-ounce) can crushed pineapple in fruit juice, undrained	Sugar to taste

Grind or chop the cranberries in a food processor. Combine the cranberries, apples, pears, pineapple and juice, oranges, orange rind, and pecans in a large bowl. Add enough sugar to suit your taste buds. Cover with plastic wrap and chill overnight. Makes about 16 servings.

⮹ Ambrosia Sour Cream ⮹

1 cup sour cream
½ cup whipping cream
½ teaspoon lemon juice

¼ cup miniature marshmallows
Fresh fruit
Flaked coconut

Combine the sour cream and whipping cream. Fold in the lemon juice and marshmallows. Spoon over fresh fruit and sprinkle with coconut. Makes about 2 cups sour cream.

⮹ Crispy Christmas Pickles ⮹

1 (46-ounce) jar whole kosher dill
  pickles, drained
1 large jar maraschino cherries,
  drained
1 tablespoon celery seed

1 tablespoon mustard seed
3 pieces cinnamon stick
4 cups sugar
1 cup vinegar

Cut pickles into thick slices. Put pickle slices and drained cherries in a large jar or glass container. Put celery seeds, mustard seeds, and cinnamon sticks in a bag (I use a double layer of coffee filters gathered at the top and tied tightly with string). Put spice bag in the jar with the pickles and cherries. Heat vinegar and sugar together almost to boiling until sugar dissolves. Carefully pour over pickles, cherries, and spice bag. Cover. When cooled, refrigerate for two days before serving. *These pickles will keep in the refrigerator for a long time.*

∽ Candied Pickles ∽

1 gallon sour pickles
Water
2 tablespoons alum powder
(purchase at drug store)
5 pounds sugar

1 box pickling spice
6 garlic buds, cut in halves or
quarters
1 cup white vinegar

Drain and cut ends off pickles. Slice pickles 1/4 inch thick and place in a large metal mixing bowl. Soak slices in the water and alum powder for 2 hours or overnight in the refrigerator. Add ice to keep cold. Pour off water. Place a 1-inch layer of sour pickles in the bottom of a gallon jar. Add a 1-inch layer of sugar. Alternate layers, sprinkling pickling spice and garlic pieces over each layer until all pickle slices and sugar are used. Pour 1 cup white vinegar into the jar; close jar lid tightly. Turn jar upside down each day until sugar is dissolved. This takes about 2 weeks. Fill 1/2-pint sterilized jars with pickles, garlic pieces, and spiced vinegar to 1/4 inch from top of jar. Seal with metal lids. Makes 12 half-pint jars. *If desired, process jars in sterilizer, or hot water covering jars, for about 15 minutes. Gingham-covered tops and fancy labels add a special touch as a gift for friends.*

THE WOMAN'S CLUB
OF NASHVILLE

There are currently 65 junior members (including two life members) and 503 senior members (including 61 life members and one honorary member). In addition to regular Bridge activities, the membership enjoys the following departments:

Education and Personal Enrichment—Programs vary and include music, foreign travel, and the history of Nashville.

Fine Arts—Programs feature local artists, musicians, and poets.

French Department—This is a serious study group that is designed to provide pleasure and fellowship.

Garden Department—Programs are designed for the true gardener and include floral design, container gardening, and historic gardens.

Great Books—This is a study group that uses Great Books Foundation material, with reviews and discussions by members.

New Horizons Department—Programs include local artists as well as speakers on education, ministry, and historic Nashville.

Potpourri Department—A very active department with 120 standing reservations, Potpourri programs include fashions, the study of investments, TV programming, opera, and gardening.

Friends Department—This is a new department formed in 1997. Members hold dinner meetings.

Junior Department—These young women are a special group. Every year they sponsor a major fund raiser, a beautiful Mother and Daughter Tea, a scholarship, a Christmas Bazaar, and Breakfast with Santa; and they decorate the clubhouse for Christmas.

◌◌ ABOUT THE CLUBHOUSE ◌◌

John Beauregard Daniel was an attorney who built three impressive homes in Nashville in the early part of this century. "Judge" Daniel (as he was called) built a stone mansion reminiscent of an Italian villa on West End Avenue. He later built a second home at the corner of Whitland and Craighead Avenues; it has a domed roof that is often compared to the roof of Thomas Jefferson's Monticello.

Then there is the lofty, white-columned Greek Revival house that Daniel built in 1929. It was purchased by The Woman's Club of Nashville in 1957 and is now the home of the club.

Judge Daniel was sometimes called "the marble mantle fancier"—he owned eighteen different marble mantles that he had collected from all over the world. The Woman's Club is fortunate to have six of these mantles.

❧ CONTRIBUTORS ❧

To create our cookbook, many excellent "member cooks" added recipes to the wonderful collection that came out of the kitchen of The Woman's Club of Nashville.

Lucille Allen
Juanita Allinder
Helen Baker
Betty K. Barnes
Anna Bauman
Suzanne Beasley
Leslie Berlin
Bette Berry
Betty M. Berry
Hannah Bird
Helen Black
Juanita T. Boyce
Sammie Boyd, Kitchen Staff
Lisa Brace
Ersel Breedlove
Beth Buchanan
Mary Budslick
Virginia Caldwell
Jean Caldwell, Kitchen Staff
Dorothy Cato
Sue Clark
Jane Davis
Janet Dickson
Allene Dillingham
Lassie Draper
Mary Driscoll
Maxine Duffey
Olga Dunbar
Margaret Dunkerley
Katherine Dunn
Lucile Edwards
Beverly Evans
Doris Fawcett

Gladys McCullough Fitzhugh
Jackie Fleming
Betty Frazer
Elsie Frazier
Martha Fulks
Anita Fuller
Helen R. Garrett
Mary Gaston
Mary Virginia Gee
Mary Goodrich
Mary Graham
Fran Greer
Marjorie Greer
Sarah Gwin
Mary Hall
Mary Katherine Hammer
Edna Claire Hardy
Lois Harper
Mary Hartnett
Dot Harvey
Annette Hicks
Ann Holland
Joyce Hollins
Margaret Hopper
Doris Horner
Kay B. Housch
Joan Huff
Lisa Hughey
Effie K. Hume
Stewart Lee Hurst
Nannie Dee James
Edna Jenkins
Geraldine Jerkins

Henrietta Johnson
Evelyn Karr
Claudette Kelton
Nelda June Kennedy
Anne Koonce
Ruth E. Koonce
Frances Kristofferson
Sarah Lamb
Elizabeth Lane
Nell Moore Lee
Virginia Lester
Genevieve D. Lish
Frances Little
Anne Elizabeth Lokey
Wendy Longmire
Mary Magee
Lisa Manning
Edna Martin
Anne Mathes
Marie Maxey
Sue McBride
Phyllis McCall
Peggy McCanless
Lou McHugh
Gibson E. McKay
Joyce McQuesten
Lynda Molteni
Lorene Moss
Mary Munn
Grace Murff
Dot Owens
Ruth Pack
Helen D. Page
Dot Pearigen
Nell Pinkerton
Sophie Plaster
Capitola Pratt
Ann Price
Dot Redman

Carole Renfro
Doris Reuther
Pat Ritter
Jean Robinson
Earline Rogers
Isabelle Ross
Bettejean Rowe
Kitty Russell
Laurine Sargent
Georgia Sasser
Willodene Scott
Ann Shaffer
Ann Singelyn
Guy Slaton
Elizabeth Smith
Betty Smith
Hazel Smith
Mary Smith
Robin Snow
Beverly St. John
Lillian Stamps
Ramona Steltemeier
Mary Stephens
Marybeth Stone
Agnes Sullivan
Alease Thompson
Dottie Threadgill
Kay Trickey
Charity Utterback
Janice Ward
Eileen Warden
Chloe Waskanin
Betty West
Nida B. Wheeler
Mil Williams
Imelda Wood
Frosty Worley
Mildred R. Wright
Normajean Wulfers

INDEX

Accompaniments. *See also* Jams and
   Preserves
Ambrosia Sour Cream, 228
Candied Pickles, 229
Crispy Christmas Pickles, 228
End of the Season Pickle, 222
Holiday Relish, 227
Appetizers. See also Dips and Spreads
Brie Appetizer, 17
Cheese and Onion Canapés, 16
Cheese Bites, 16
Cocktail Oyster Crackers, 18
Crescent Roll Appetizers, 15
Deviled Ham and Cheese Snacks, 17
Greek Cheese Triangles, 18
Ham and Cheese Rolls, 20
Olive Balls, 15
Open-Faced Ham Biscuits, 20
Oyster Cracker Munchies, 19
Ranch Pinwheels, 19
Beans
Barbecued Green Beans, 98
Bean Bundles, 97
Good Quick Green Beans, 97
Louisiana-Style Red Beans and
   Rice, 116
Western Baked Beans, 104
Beef. See also Ground Beef
Beef Burgundy, 63
Beef Pimento with Horseradish
   Sauce, 61
Beef Roast, 57
Beef Stew, 57
Holiday Beef Ribeye Roast, 62
Spicy Texas Chili, 58
Veal Loaf, 56
Beverages
Fruit Punch, 29
Hot Spiced Tea Mix, 30
Iced Spiced Tea, 30
Rich and Creamy Coffee Punch, 28
Strawberry Punch, 29
Yellow Punch, 28
Breads. *See also* Corn Bread; Muffins
Banana Nut Bread, 141
Buttermilk Biscuits, 123
Carrot Bread, 138
Cheese Biscuits, 132
Dilly Bread, 125

English Muffin Bread, 129
Fancy Biscuits, 131
Lemon Poppy Seed Loaves, 139
Nut Cheese Bread Sticks, 132
Oatmeal Yeast Rolls, 124
Parker House Refrigerator Rolls, 126
Poppy Seed Bread, 139
Pumpkin Bread, 141
Quick Biscuits, 131
Quick Coffee Cake, 133
Ruth's Pumpkin Bread, 140
Salt Rising Bread, 122
Sour Cream Coffee Cake, 134
Spoon Rolls, 128
Strawberry Bread, 134
Strawberry Nut Bread, 135
Broccoli
Broccoli Casserole, 112
Broccoli-Cheddar Corn Bread, 127
Broccoli Corn Bake, 113
Broccoli Corn Bread, 127
Swiss Broccoli, 97
Cakes
Amaretto Cake, 154
Apple Cake, 155
Apple Cake II, 157
Best Cheesecake, 167
Butter Cake, 145
Buttermilk Cake, 154
Buttermilk Pound Cake, 163
Carrot Cake, 145
Chocolate Cherry Cake, 161
Chocolate Pound Cake, 165
Coconut Cake, 149
Coconut Macaroon Cheesecake, 168
Coconut Pound Cake, 166
Cream Cheese Pound Cake, 164
Delectable Cheesecake, 169
Earthquake Cake, 151
Five-Flavor Cake, 152
Fresh Apple Cake, 156
Fresh Apple Nut Cake, 156
German Sweet Chocolate Cake, 172
Glory Be Cake, 175
Hummingbird Cake, 171
Italian Cream Cake, 170
Jam Cake, 152
Lemon Daffodil Torte, 174
Lemon Pound Cake, 163

"Lindsey" Chocolate Chip Bundt
Cake, 151
Mississippi Mud Cake, 169
Mother's White Fruit Cake, 161
Old-Fashioned Fruit Cake, 159
Ooie Gooie Butter Cake, 148
Orange Chiffon Cake, 173
Piña Colada Cake, 147
Pineapple Nut Cake, 162
Pound Cake, 164
Prune Cake, 176
Pumpkin Cake, 162
Raspberry-Walnut Torte, 153
7-Up Cake, 147
Snowball Cake, 158
Sock It to Me Cake, 146
Sour Cream Coconut Cake, 157
Spicy Fruit Cake, 160
Spicy Gingerbread with Lemon
Sauce, 150
Strawberry Cake, 175
Tennessee Black Walnut Cake, 148
Texas Tornado Cake, 175
Triple Chocolate Cake, 149
Vasilopita, 155
Wine-Pecan Cake, 159
World Famous Peach Cake, 146

Candy
Bourbon Balls, 216
Confection Bites, 217
Crystallized Pecans, 219
Divinity, 219
Heath Bar Candy, 218
Microwave Peanut Brittle, 217
Peanut Butter Balls, 220
Peanut Butter Cups, 220
Peanut Butter Fudge, 216
Pralines, 218

Chicken. *See also* Turkey
Buttered Chicken with Potatoes, 77
Chicken à la King, 88
Chicken Almond Casserole, 80
Chicken and Rice Casserole, 78
Chicken and Saffron Rice, 76
Chicken Breasts with Wine
Sauce, 85
Chicken Casserole, 78
Chicken Enchilada Pie, 83
Chicken Monterey, 81
Chicken Teriyaki, 76
Chicken Tetrazzini, 84

Grilled Rosemary
Chicken, 80
Herbed Chicken en Casserole, 85
Hot Brown, 87
Hot Chicken Salad 79,
Hot Chicken Salad II, 83
Luncheon Chicken Casserole, 82
Oriental Chicken with Cheese
Soufflé, 86
Poppy Seed Chicken, 77

Cookies and Bars
Basic Sugar Cookies, 206
Brown Sugar Brownies, 200
Butterscotch Bars, 203
Butterscotch Delight, 204
Cranberry Crunch Bars, 201
Chess Cake Cookies, 200
Chess Cake Squares, 204
Chocolate Chip Cookies, 208
Date Skillet Cookies, 201
Delicious Brownies, 203
Fruitcake Cookies, 197
Graham Cracker Toffee Bars, 202
Hello Dollys, 203
No-Bake Chocolate Oatmeal
Cookies, 206
Oatmeal Cookies, 198
Oatmeal-Raisin Cookies, 208
Orange Coconut Balls, 202
Peanut Butter Cookies, 197
Pecan Puffs, 210
Scottish Shortbread, 199
Snow Drops, 198
Tea Cakes, 207
The State Cookie of Tennessee, 205
Toffee Bars, 216
Vanilla Sugar Cookies, 207
Zasu's Delicious Oatmeal
Cookies, 199

Corn
Broccoli Corn Bake, 113
Corn Casserole, 99
Mamma's Corn Pudding, 100
Quick Corn, 98
Shoe Peg Corn Casserole, 99

Corn Bread
Broccoli Corn Bread, 127
Broccoli-Cheddar Corn Bread, 127
Corn Muffins, 125
Corn Bread, 129
Egg Corn Bread, 128

Hush Puppies, 124
Jalapeño Corn Bread, 123
Mexican Corn Bread, 130
Sour Cream Corn Bread, 130
Desserts. *See also* Cakes; Candy;
    Cookies; Pies; Sauces, Dessert
Banana Pudding, 212
Bananas Foster, 213
Brandied Orange Custard, 209
Butterhorns, 211
Chocolate Mousse, 214
Danish Pudding, 209
"Death by Chocolate" Truffle, 213
French Apple Cobbler, 195
Jam Pudding, 144
Layered Lemon Gelatin, 214
Old-Fashioned Boiled Custard, 210
Orange Crush Sherbet, 215
Peach Cobbler, 195
Strawberry Parfait, 211
Watkins Country-Style Vanilla Ice
    Cream, 215
Dips and Spreads
Artichoke Dip, 23
Black-Eyed Pea Salsa, 25
Congealed Corned Beef Spread, 21
Dawn's Apricot Cream Cheese
    Log, 22
Fish Mold Spread, 26
Hot Chipped Beef Dip, 23
Layered Cheese Paté, 27
Pimento Cheese, 224
Shrimp Dip, 22
Spicy Beef Dip, 26
Spinach-Crab Dip, 21
Spinach Dip, 24
Summer Salsa, 24
Vegetable Dip, 25
Egg Dishes
Cheese Soufflé, 86
Swiss Eggs, 117
Frostings and Icings
Buttermilk Icing, 176
Chocolate Icing, 165, 177
Coconut-Pecan Frosting, 173
Cream Cheese Frosting, 170, 171
Creamy White Frosting, 174
Easy Caramel Icing, 176
Five-Flavor Glaze, 152
Never-Fail Frosting, 177

Ground Beef
Beef Tomato Casserole, 59
Chili, 57
Dinner-in-a-Dish, 64
Eggplant Casserole, 65
Favorite Meat Loaf, 64
Johnny Mosetti, 66
Mexi-Corn Lasagna, 60
Mitzi's Chili, 59
Saucy Manicotti, 67
Small Meatballs, 63
Texas Hash, 65
Jams and Preserves
Cranberry Jam, 225
Frozen Strawberry Preserves, 224
Holiday Jam, 225
Lamb
Lamb and Carrot Meatballs, 75
Lamb Curry, 75
Muffins
All-Bran Muffins, 136
Bran Muffins, 135
Corn Muffins, 125
Plum Muffins, 137
Pumpkin Muffins, 140
Sweet Potato Muffins, 137
Zucchini Muffins, 142
Pasta
Chicken Tetrazzini, 84
Green Noodle Casserole, 89
Linguine with Tomatoes and
    Artichoke Hearts, 117
Macaroni and Cheese, 118
Saucy Manicotti, 67
Pie Crusts
Crunchy Pie Crust, 196
Never-Fail Pie Crust, 196
Press 'n' Bake Crust, 184
Pies
Almond Pecan Pie, 178
Ann's Fudge Pie, 178
Apple Pie, 181
Blueberry Pie, 180
Buttermilk Pie, 182
Caramel Pie, 190
Chess Pie, 183
Chess Pie II, 185
Chocolate Brownie Pie, 185
Chocolate Chess Tarts, 186
Chocolate Chip Pecan Pie, 180

Chocolate Chip Pie, 192
Chocolate Pie, 193
Coconut Oatmeal Pie, 183
Creamy Lemon Filling, 196
Derby Pie, 192
Derby Pie II, 192
French Coconut Pie, 178
French Raisin Pie, 189
Hershey Bar Pie, 182
Impossible Pumpkin Pie, 187
Japanese Fruit Pie, 189
Lemon Meringue Pie, 194
Lemonade Pie, 181
Margarita Pie, 188
Margarita Pretzel Pie, 188
Millionaire Pie, 179
No-Crust Fudge Pie, 193
Peanut Butter Ice Cream Pie, 191
Peanut Butter Pie, 190
Peanut Butter Refrigerator Pie, 191
Pecan Pie, 178, 179, 180
Pumpkin Chess Pie, 184
Pumpkin Chiffon Pie, 187
Pumpkin Pie, 186
Strawberry Pie, 194
Pork
Apricot-Glazed Pork Roast, 74
Barbecued Pork Chops, 68
Betty Ham Recipe, 69
Favorite Meat Loaf, 64
Ham and Cheese Quiche, 69
Honey Pork Oriental, 70
Jezebel Sauce for Pork
Tenderloin, 223
Marinade for Pork Tenderloin, 223
Quiche Lorraine, 70
Ribs and Kraut, 72
Rice-Stuffed Ham Rolls with
Mushroom Cheese Sauce, 71
Sausage and Rice Casserole, 71
Sausage Casserole, 68
Snowballs, 72
Spinach Quiche, 74
Potatoes
Company Potatoes, 108
Hash Brown Potato Casserole, 109
Potato Casserole, 106
Stuffed Baked Potatoes, 107
Quiches
Crustless Quiche, 73
Ham and Cheese Quiche, 69

Quiche Lorraine, 70
Spinach Quiche, 74
Rice
Carrots and Rice, 96
Cheese Rice, 115
Chicken and Rice Casserole, 78
Chicken and Saffron Rice, 76
Chili Cheese Rice, 116
Green Rice, 115
Louisiana-Style Red Beans and
Rice, 116
Rice-Stuffed Ham Rolls with
Mushroom Cheese Sauce, 71
Sausage and Rice Casserole, 71
Snowballs, 72
Salad Dressings
Blueberry Poppy Seed Dressing, 227
Curry French Dressing, 226
Salad Dressing for Fruit, 226
Sweet-Sour French Dressing, 226
Salads, Fruit
Buttermilk Salad, 50
Chicken and Fruit Salad, 38
Cinnamon Applesauce Swirl
Salad, 54
Coke Salad, 42
Cranberry Salad, 35
Curried Fruit, 49
Five-Cup Salad, 53
Frozen Cherry Salad, 48
Frozen Fruit Salad, 32, 50
Fruit Cup, 51
Fruit Salad, 51
Lime-Pear Salad, 37
Mango Salad, 52
Orange Sherbet Gelatin Salad, 37
Orange Sherbet Salad, 49
Peach Salad, 53
Pineapple Lime Salad, 36
Pink Arctic Freeze, 35
Purple Lady Salad, 54
Spiced Peach Salad, 52
Salads, Main Dish
Chicken and Fruit Salad, 38
Mediterranean Pasta Salad, 47
Party Chicken Pie Salad, 38
Salads, Vegetable
Carrot Salad, 45
Coleslaw, 42
Congealed Asparagus Salad, 41
Congealed Cabbage Slaw, 44

Golden Glow Salad, 48
Green Pea Salad, 39
Layered Potato Salad, 36
Marinated Tomato Slices, 40
Marinated Tomatoes, 41
Molded Cucumber Aspic, 40
Pea Salad, 44
Spring Tonic Salad, 46
Three-Bean Salad, 47
Tomato Aspic, 39
Tomato Salad, 39
Tomato Soup Salad, 46
Twenty-Four Hour Cole Slaw, 43
Twenty-Four Hour Salad, 43
Vegetable Salad, 45
Sauces
Barbecue Sauce, 223
Holiday Currant Sauce, 62
Jezebel Sauce for Pork
    Tenderloin, 223
Marinade for Pork Tenderloin, 223
White Sauce, 67
Sauces, Dessert
Lemon Sauce, 150
Raspberry Sauce, 153
Vanilla Sauce, 224
Seafood
Classy Crab Meat Casserole, 91
Hot Crab Sandwich, 92
Olsen's Shrimp and Egg Creole
    Casserole, 94
Oysters, 14
Salmon Loaf, 91, 93
Shrimp au Gratin Supreme, 93
Shrimp Crab Meat Casserole, 92
Side Dishes
Dried Fruit Casserole, 119
Grits Casserole, 119
Hot Fruit, 120
Pineapple Delight, 119
Yummy Fruit Casserole, 120
Soups
Cabbage and Beef Soup, 34
Lentil Soup, 33
Spicy Tortilla Soup, 33
Vegetable Beef Soup, 34
Squash
Baked Acorn Squash, 102

Company Coming Squash
    Casserole, 105
Squash Casserole, 104
Sweet Potatoes
Rich Sweet Potato Casserole, 101
Sweet Potato Muffins, 137
Sweet Potatoes, 100
Sweet Potatoes Caramel, 101
Tomatoes
Beef Tomato Casserole, 59
Granny's Okra and Tomatoes, 110
Linguine with Tomatoes and
    Artichoke Hearts, 117
Marinated Tomatoes, 41
Marinated Tomato Slices, 40
Stuffed Tomatoes with Lamb and
    Feta, 118
Tomato Aspic, 39
Tomato Salad, 39
Tomato Soup Salad, 46
Turkey
Green Noodle Casserole, 89
Hot Brown, 87
Hot Turkey Hustle Up, 88
Puff Top Turkey Sandwiches, 82
Turkey Black Bean Chili, 90
Turkey Divan, 89
Vegetables. *See also* individual types
Asparagus Casserole, 102
Asparagus Casserole II, 103
Beets, 106
Cabbage Casserole, 113
Carrots and Rice, 96
Fried Eggplant, 99
Fried Onion Rings, 114
Granny's Okra and Tomatoes, 110
Hoppin' John, 103
Marinated Carrots, 114
Marinated Mushrooms, 108
Mixed Vegetables Casserole, 112
Peas Vinaigrette, 98
Spinach Casserole, 111
Spinach Souffle, 111
Stuffed Tomatoes with Lamb and
    Feta, 118
Veg-All Casserole, 109
Vegetable Medley, 105

The Woman's Club of Nashville

3206 Hillsboro Road
Nashville, TN 37215-1575
(615) 269-3896

Favorite Recipes from the Kitchen
Order Form

Please send _____ copies of *The Woman's Club of Nashville Cookbook* at $19.95 plus $3.00 shipping and handling ($22.95) for each copy. Enclosed is my check or money order to The Woman's Club of Nashville for $_____.

_____ **copy(ies) to:**

Name _____

Address _____

City_____ State_____ Zip _____

Phone (_____) _____

_____ **copy(ies) to:**

Name _____

Address _____

City_____ State_____ Zip _____

Phone (_____) _____

_____ **copy(ies) to:**

Name _____

Address _____

City_____ State_____ Zip _____

Phone (_____) _____